Especially for

....

From

....

Date

....

ISBN 978-1-64352-165-7

Daily entries are taken from the following Spiritual Refreshment for Women titles, published by Barbour Publishing, Inc.: *Everyday Blessings*, *Everyday Comfort*, *Everyday Encouragement*, *Everyday Hope*, *Everyday Joy*, *Everyday Prayers*, *Everyday Promises*, and *Everyday Wisdom*.

Published by Barbour Books, an imprint of Barbour Publishing, Inc., 1810 Barbour Drive, Uhrichsville, Ohio 44683, www.barbourbooks.com

Our mission is to inspire the world with the life-changing message of the Bible.

Member of the
Evangelical Christian
Publishers Association

Printed in China.

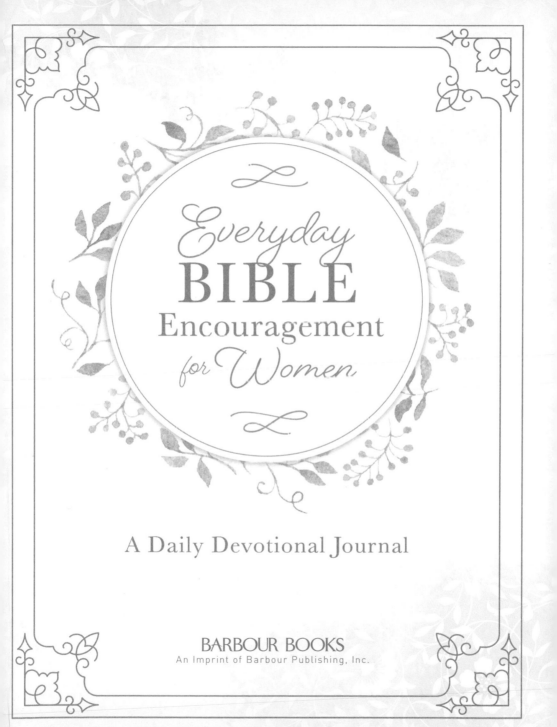

Everyday BIBLE Encouragement for Women

A Daily Devotional Journal

BARBOUR BOOKS
An Imprint of Barbour Publishing, Inc.

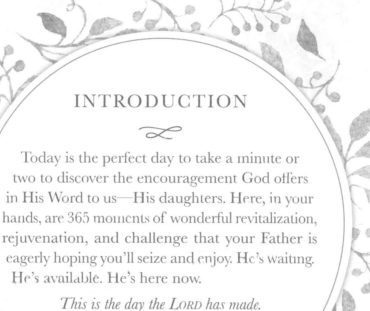

INTRODUCTION

Today is the perfect day to take a minute or two to discover the encouragement God offers in His Word to us—His daughters. Here, in your hands, are 365 moments of wonderful revitalization, rejuvenation, and challenge that your Father is eagerly hoping you'll seize and enjoy. He's waiting. He's available. He's here now.

This is the day the LORD has made.
We will rejoice and be glad in it.
PSALM 118:24 NLT

EVERYDAY JOY

The joy of the Lord is your strength.
NEHEMIAH 8:10 KJV

Is it really possible to have joy in your everyday life—even when the kids are crying and the bills are piling up? When you're overwhelmed with work or struggling with emotional problems? Can you truly "rejoice and be glad" in the midst of such trials? Of course you can! Rejoicing is a choice, and it's one the Lord hopes you'll make in every situation. His joy will give you the strength you need to make it through. So, rejoice, dear one. Rejoice!

....

....

....

....

....

....

....

....

....

....

....

....

....

....

ACCEPTANCE

To get wisdom is to love oneself; to keep understanding is to prosper.
PROVERBS 19:8 NRSV

If you can accept yourself, you will probably be more readily able to accept the idiosyncrasies of others. If you are patient with yourself, you will almost certainly be more tolerant toward your loved ones. If you have learned to forgive yourself, you're likely to find you can more easily forgive someone else. Self-respect increases as you stay committed to gaining a heart of wisdom. This attitude splashes onto your other relationships, and acceptance gradually becomes a way of life.

Day 3

A PRAYER FOR MY CHILDREN

"If you believe, you will receive whatever you ask for in prayer."
Matthew 21:22

Just the other day, someone reminded me of how important it is to pray for my children. So here I am, Lord. Please protect my kids. Work in their lives so that they will want to serve You with body, mind, and soul. Provide the things they need, and fill them with contentment as they bask in the warmth of Your love.

Day 4

I WILL FOLLOW YOU

Direct my footsteps according to your word; let no sin rule over me.
PSALM 119:133

My son leaves little footprints as he exits the pool and walks across the cement. Even as I follow him, they fade. Lord, You also left footprints. Yet because of the Bible, because of learned teachers, and because of an intense desire to follow You, we can still see Your footsteps—instead of fading, they become bolder.

....

....

....

....

....

....

....

....

....

....

....

....

....

EVERY SINGLE ONE

We have different gifts, according to the grace given to each of us.
ROMANS 12:6

God has blessed every person—every single one—with some gift or ability with which to serve others and bring glory to His name. Some abilities are obvious—they shine brightly in front of everyone—but others move below the radar. They include such things as the ability to pray effectively, love the unlovely, and listen attentively. Ask God to open your eyes to your special abilities. They are God's blessings to you.

EVERYDAY BLESSINGS

But the eyes of the Lord are on those who fear him,
on those whose hope is in his unfailing love.

PSALM 33:18

The Lord of all creation is watching our every moment and wants to fill us with His joy. He often interrupts our lives with His blessings: butterflies dancing in sunbeams, dew-touched spiderwebs, cotton-candy clouds, and glorious crimson sunsets. The beauty of His creation reassures us of His unfailing love and fills us with hope. But it is up to us to take the time to notice.

....

....

....

....

....

....

....

....

....

....

....

THE GOD OF ALL COMFORT

*"Do not fear or be dismayed; tomorrow go out
against them, for the LORD is with you."*
2 CHRONICLES 20:17 NKJV

Adversity, calamity, hardship, misfortune, trouble—no matter what you call it, painful episodes are part and parcel of the human experience. But you can choose not to let them bring you down, fill you with fear, and steal your attention from the blessings God has placed in your life. Look adversity square in the eye, and know that your God—the God of all comfort—has an answer.

....

....

....

....

....

....

....

....

....

....

....

POWERFUL PRAYER

*"The LORD bless you and keep you; the LORD make
his face shine on you and be gracious to you."*
NUMBERS 6:24–25

Want to pray for someone? This is a good way to do it. It's the blessing God gave Aaron and his sons to pronounce on Israel. What Christian wouldn't appreciate these words committing her to God's care and wanting her to draw closer to Him? Who would turn down the good things God has to offer? Can you bless your friends and family with these thoughts today?

....

....

....

....

....

....

....

....

....

....

....

Day 9

BUBBLING JOY

Can both fresh water and salt water flow from the same spring?
JAMES 3:11

Can you feel it—that bubbling in your midsection? Can you sense it rising to the surface? Joy comes from the deepest place inside of us, so deep that we often forget it's there at all. Wonder of wonders! It rises up, up, up to the surface, and the most delightful thing happens. Troubles vanish. Sorrows disappear. Godly joy has the power to squelch negative emotions. So let the bubbling begin!

_____

_____

_____

_____

_____

_____

_____

_____

_____

_____

_____

_____

BEAUTY IN YOU

Humans are satisfied with whatever looks good; GOD probes for what is good.
PROVERBS 16:2 MSG

Like many women, you probably enjoy looking nice when you go out for a special occasion. You want a hairstyle that flatters your face, clothes that fit well, and a little makeup to enhance your eyes and cheeks. God likes it when you feel good about your appearance, but He cares more about the inner you. He wants to cultivate what's good about you socially, emotionally, mentally, and spiritually. Join with Him in cultivating the beauty that's inside you.

....

....

....

....

....

....

....

....

....

....

....

....

Day 11

GOD-HONORING ACTIVITIES

May Jesus himself and God our Father, who reached out in love and surprised you with gifts of unending help and confidence, put a fresh heart in you, invigorate your work, enliven your speech.
2 THESSALONIANS 2:17 MSG

There are many ways to be involved in my community, Father, and I ask You to show me what to do. I want to choose activities that will help others and bring glory to You. Help me to weigh the possibilities carefully and to make the best decisions. Thank You for these opportunities to honor You.

....

....

....

....

....

....

....

....

....

....

....

....

....

RATED G

*"Choose for yourselves this
day whom you will serve."*
Joshua 24:15

The newspaper is spread out before us and opened to the movie listings. Have movies changed? Or have we changed? Most of the movies we've never heard of. The others are ones we don't want to see. Change is an interesting concept. We either run toward it or we never see it coming. In this case, age has made us not only older but wiser. Some of these movies do not deserve an audience. Thank You, Father, for letting us grow into the knowledge that we need to feed our minds with what is good and pure.

FULLY SATISFIED

The desires of the diligent are fully satisfied.
PROVERBS 13:4

It's a fact of life that you don't always get what you want. You've been learning that lesson since you were two and the floor wasn't too far away to stage a tantrum. But now that you are pretty far from the floor, you have to remember that there's a difference between having everything you want and being satisfied. God doesn't promise to fulfill your every craving, but if you live life in a relationship with Him, you will be satisfied—fully satisfied.

SMILING IN THE DARKNESS

"The hopes of the godless evaporate."
JOB 8:13 NLT

Hope isn't just an emotion; it's a perspective, a discipline, a way of life. It's a journey of choice. We must learn to override those messages of discouragement, despair, and fear that assault us in times of trouble and press toward the light. Hope is smiling in the darkness. It's confidence that faith in God's sovereignty amounts to something—something life changing, life saving, and eternal.

....

....

....

....

....

....

....

....

....

....

....

....

....

....

....

....

FAR GREATER MEASURE

[Jesus said,] "Give, and it will be given to you. A good measure, pressed down, shaken together and running over, will be poured into your lap. For with the measure you use, it will be measured to you."
LUKE 6:38

If you want more, give more. That's God's way, and He invites you to make it your way too. He promises you abundance when you generously share your time, efforts, resources, and abilities. Do so without expecting a reward, knowing all along that God will reward you in far greater measure than you can imagine. Give His way a try, and find out for yourself.

....

....

....

....

....

....

....

....

....

....

....

LOOK TO THE SHEPHERD

The Lord is my shepherd, I lack nothing.
PSALM 23:1

No matter what your physical circumstances, if Jesus is your Shepherd, you never have to want spiritually. No matter what the world throws at you, you can be at peace. No fear overcomes those who follow the Shepherd as their King. He guides them through every trial, leading them faithfully into an eternity with Him. Are you lacking contentment today? Look to the Shepherd for peace.

....
....
....
....
....
....
....
....
....
....
....
....
....
....

JOYFUL OBEDIENCE

*Now unto him that is able to keep you from falling, and to present you
faultless before the presence of his glory with exceeding joy.*
JUDE 1:24 KJV

Our obedience makes God happy—and should make us happy too. In
fact, the more difficult it is to obey, the more joyful we should be. Why?
Because a big situation calls for a big God. And our God is bigger than
anything we could ask or think. He alone can prevent us from falling. So
if you're struggling in the area of obedience, surrender your will. Enter
into joyful obedience.

....

....

....

....

....

....

....

....

....

....

....

....

Day 18

AUTHENTICITY

The LORD looks deep inside people
and searches through their thoughts.
PROVERBS 20:27 NCV

If you're like most women who have participated in relationship surveys, you want someone to hear your heart and not run away. Although you may have been disappointed in relationships before, you still desire to be loved for who you really are. Good news! God is not surprised by what you feel, say, or think. He knows you inside and out and loves you just the way you are. So drop your guard and be authentic with Him. He isn't going anywhere.

Day 19

JOSHUA'S EXAMPLE

*Jesus said to him, "If you can believe,
all things are possible to him who believes."*
MARK 9:23 NKJV

Joshua faced a tough challenge, didn't he, Lord? He had to get a rather difficult group of people across a flooding river, and that was merely the beginning. But he didn't flinch. He trusted Your promises, and I can too. Thank You for reminding me of Joshua's example when I needed it most.

....

....

....

....

....

....

....

....

....

....

....

....

....

....

Day 20

CURL UP NEXT TO THE HEARTH

*For in the day of trouble he will keep me safe
in his dwelling; he will hide me in the shelter of
his sacred tent and set me high upon a rock.*

PSALM 27:5

The rain pours down from the heavens. Batting a tentative paw against the screen door, the cat finds unexpected freedom and runs out into the dampness. He makes it a few feet before coldness, wind, and wetness stop him in his tracks. *This is not freedom!* He races back inside to the warmth of his master's home. Lord, if only we reacted to sin the way that cat reacted to rain! Help us always to turn our hearts in the direction of Your heavenly mansion.

....

....

....

....

....

....

....

....

....

....

GO FOR IT!

A longing fulfilled is a tree of life.
PROVERBS 13:12

You are a fortunate woman! You live in a time when women can accomplish anything they set their minds to do. Will you still face obstacles? Of course, but nothing you can't deal with. God has given you something special to do in this world. You'll know it by the longing you feel deep inside. Ask God to guide you, lending you His wisdom, grace, and strength. Then go for it. Nothing can compare with the joy of accomplishing God's will for your life.

....

....

....

....

....

....

....

....

....

....

....

STOP THE ROLLER COASTER

*Why am I discouraged? Why is my heart
so sad? I will put my hope in God!*
PSALM 43:5 NLT

Careening hormones often cause ruts of depression for women. We spend countless hours weeping without knowing why. Or we bite someone's head off, lose precious sleep, or sprout funky nervous habits. Knowing that this hormonally crazed state is only temporary, we must intentionally place our hope in tomorrow and pray that God will turn the downside up!

....

....

....

....

....

....

....

....

....

....

....

....

....

....

ETERNAL LIFE

*[Jesus said,] "Very truly I tell you, whoever hears my word
and believes him who sent me has eternal life and will not
be judged but has crossed over from death to life."*
JOHN 5:24

When you're tempted to live for the moment, consider this: God has
given you eternal life right now. God means for you to give up a human,
shortsighted perspective and live as if you're living for eternity—because
you are. Ask God to allow His Spirit to stretch your spiritual sight beyond
this moment. Let Him show you what matters for all eternity; then commit
yourself to live in it.

KINGDOM-PURPOSED FRIENDSHIP

*"I tell you, use worldly wealth to gain friends
for yourselves, so that when it is gone, you will
be welcomed into eternal dwellings."*

LUKE 16:9

Jesus describes a good way to use the things of the world. God has given us wealth so that we can further God's kingdom by sharing with others. Though we may not have more than a pot of soup and some bread to offer, these things can be the start of a kingdom-purposed friendship. What do you have that God can use in this way?

....

....

....

....

....

....

....

....

....

....

....

....

EVERYDAY JOY

For in him we live, and move,
and have our being.
ACTS 17:28 KJV

Every breath we breathe comes from God. Every step we take is a gift from our Creator. We can do nothing apart from Him. In the same sense, every joy, every sorrow—God goes through each one with us. His heart is for us. We can experience joy in our everyday lives even when things aren't going our way. We simply have to remember that He is in control. We have our being— in Him!

Day 26

A BEAUTIFUL CREATION

"She'll garland your life with grace,
she'll festoon your days with beauty."

PROVERBS 4:9 MSG

You are a beautiful creation of God. As a woman with a heart for God, you seek wisdom and understanding. And it shows. Grace is reflected in your eyes as you speak with kindness and encouragement. Magazine advertisements and Hollywood may tell you that to be one of the "beautiful people" you must maintain an ideal weight, banish wrinkles, schedule regular pedicures, highlight your hair—and more. While all these regimens are fine, wisdom's loveliness far exceeds them all.

....

....

....

....

....

....

....

....

....

....

....

....

....

....

A NEW CHALLENGE EACH DAY

*Such things were written in the Scriptures long
ago to teach us. And the Scriptures give us hope
and encouragement as we wait patiently
for God's promises to be fulfilled.*

ROMANS 15:4 NLT

Oh how I enjoy a good challenge, Lord, and each day challenges me anew!
Thank You for these opportunities—for each exciting adventure. My desire
is that I might face each task in a godly manner, and that I might honor You
in all I say and do.

WHAT WE REALLY WANT

*And there appeared before them Elijah
and Moses, who were talking with Jesus.*
MARK 9:4

Moses and Elijah? Appearing years after their deaths and talking with Jesus? Amazing. I used to feel sorry for Moses. To think that he led the people, walked for years, and yet was denied the promised land here on earth. But he truly spoke with and walked with God. The promised land of milk and honey pales in comparison to heaven. Oh Father, what joy to know that someday we will talk and walk with Jesus!

....

....

....

....

....

....

....

....

....

....

....

....

Day 29

FOR GENERATIONS

All thy children shall be taught of the LORD;
and great shall be the peace of thy children.
ISAIAH 54:13 KJV

There is no heritage like the knowledge of God's love—no inheritance as empowering. As you live your life of faith before your family, it is like stocking a vault that will bless everyone. And it is never too late to begin. Live authentically before God, and you will leave a blueprint for those who are watching. That example can last for generations—it is more influential than you can fathom.

LORD OF THE DANCE

Remember your promise to me; it is my only hope.
Psalm 119:49 nlt

The Bible contains many promises from God: He will protect us (Proverbs 1:33), comfort us (2 Corinthians 1:5), help us in our times of trouble (Psalm 46:1), and encourage us (Isaiah 40:29). The word *encourage* comes from the root phrase "to inspire courage." Like an earthly father who encourages his daughter during her dance recital, our Papa God wants to inspire courage in us, if we only look to Him.

Day 31

MOTIVES

*"Serve him with wholehearted devotion and with
a willing mind, for the LORD searches every heart
and understands every desire and every thought."*
1 CHRONICLES 28:9

We publicly claim that we are not asking for a reward but then privately seek acclaim when no reward comes our way. If you find yourself harboring offense, check the motives behind your charitable acts—God already has. Ask Him to replace selfish motives with selfless ones and to instill in you a spirit of compassion, kindness, and generosity. On the outside, you'll continue doing the good things you've been doing. On the inside, you'll be doing them for the right reasons.

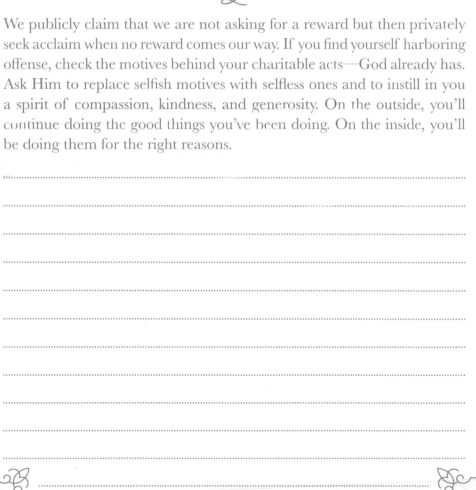

SAFE IN HIS WILL

Your hand will guide me,
your right hand will hold me fast.
PSALM 139:10

Do you need to make a life-changing decision? God wants to be part of it. As the psalmist understood, allowing God to guide your steps means you won't get off track and land in a nasty situation. The best place for a believer to be is in the palm of God's hand, safe from harm and in the center of His will.

....

....

....

....

....

....

....

....

....

....

....

....

....

JOY IN SERVING

So we, being many, are one body in Christ,
and every one members one of another.
ROMANS 12:5 KJV

There's a lot of work to be done in the local church. Someone has to teach the children, vacuum the floors, prepare meals for the sick, and so forth. With so many needs, how does the body of Christ function without its various members feeling taken advantage of? If you're in a position of service at your local church, praise God for the opportunity to serve others. Step out—with joy leading the way.

Day 34

HONORABLE

[God] loves it when business is aboveboard.
PROVERBS 11:1 MSG

Whether you're a stay-at-home mother, empty nester, CEO, student, teacher, or attorney, God expects you to be honest. Honest in all your transactions—at the grocery store, the local bank, with your children and husband, in the boardroom, in court, on your tax forms, and with your repair person. Maybe you had trustworthy role models when you were growing up; perhaps you didn't. But as an aspiring wise woman, you *can* keep your everyday business dealings honorable. God will help.

....

....

....

....

....

....

....

....

....

....

....

Day 35

MATCHLESS GRACE

For thou, Lord, art good, and ready to forgive;
and plenteous in mercy unto all
them that call upon thee.
PSALM 86:5 KJV

The song talks of praising You for Your matchless grace, and how could I go through a single day without doing so? I don't understand why You love and forgive me, but I wish to offer my sincerest thanks for these bountiful gifts. You are a wonderful Savior!

Day 36

OPEN YOUR EARS

I will listen to what God the Lord says; he promises peace to his people,
his faithful servants—but let them not turn to folly.

Psalm 85:8

I was in my thirties before I understood the parable of the prodigal son. Before that, I wholeheartedly understood the older son's quandary. Ironically, in life, I was the prodigal son. Lord, I'm so thankful for the lessons of learned teachers. As I grow in Your knowledge, I understand more about the importance of keeping my feet firmly on the path to redemption.

....

....

....

....

....

....

....

....

....

....

....

....

....

CONNECTED

If we walk in the light, as he is in the light,
we have fellowship with one another.
1 JOHN 1:7

Living in a close relationship with God empowers you to connect with people meaningfully. As you grow toward Him, you will find yourself growing in your relationships with others as well. This comes as a result of having the same heavenly Father, living in the same kingdom, and sharing the same destination—heaven. Enjoy the great spiritual family God has placed you in—the family of faith. Be there for your family members, and let them be there for you. That is what God intended.

....

....

....

....

....

....

....

....

....

....

....

FEEL THE LOVE

Long before he laid down earth's foundations,
he had us in mind, had settled on us as the focus
of his love, to be made whole and holy by his love.

EPHESIANS 1:4 MSG

Need a boost of hope today? Read this passage aloud, inserting your name for each "us." Wow! Doesn't that bring home the message of God's amazing, extravagant, customized love for you? I am the focus of His love, and I bask in the hope of healing, wholeness, and holiness that His individualized attention brings. You too, dear sister, are His focus. Allow yourself to feel the love today.

....

....

....

....

....

....

....

....

....

....

GROWING PAINS

Confess your faults one to another,
and pray one for another, that ye may be healed.
JAMES 5:16 KJV

Criticism hurts. While your first reaction is, quite naturally, to retaliate, God has an alternative in mind. He says to listen to the words of your critic. If someone has pinpointed a fault in your conduct or character, give thanks that you have someone in your life who is frank and truthful enough to tell you where you need to make changes. Ask the Holy Spirit to help you mature and grow in this area.

AVAILABLE 24-7

*"Blessed is the man to whom
the Lord shall not impute sin."*

ROMANS 4:8 NKJV

Our sin is forgiven—what a wonderful thought! No longer do we need to be dragged into wrongdoing, because God has cleansed our hearts. His Spirit sweeps through us, lifting the burden of sin from our lives. Though we still fail, in Christ, God will not hold the sin against us. Forgiveness, available 24-7, sends His Spirit through our lives again and again.

WITH THANKSGIVING

I will praise the name of God with a song,
and will magnify him with thanksgiving.
PSALM 69:30 KJV

It's one thing to spend time with God; it's another to praise Him with a thankful heart. Sometimes we forget His many blessings. We praise out of routine. Today allow God to remind you of the many ways He has blessed you. Oh what full and thankful hearts we have when we pause to remember. Now watch your praises rise to the surface like cream to the top of the pitcher.

Day 42

RUSH AND HURRY

One who moves too hurriedly misses the way.
<small>PROVERBS 19:2 NRSV</small>

Hurry. Faster. Accomplish more. Learn this. Study that. Time's wasting. Do more for God. Messages like these fly around us daily—whether they're blatant or inferred. Perhaps you've sensed the rush and have become too busy trying to do it all. Now you're tired. How can you change? First, know that God isn't the one pressing the hurry button. He doesn't want you to dash through life and lose your way. He wants you to slow down and enjoy every minute.

Day 43

THANK YOU FOR THE LIGHTNING BUGS

I will praise thee, O LORD, with my whole heart;
I will shew forth all thy marvellous works.
PSALM 9:1 KJV

I am convinced, Father, that one reason You bring children across our paths is to teach us important lessons. It wasn't long ago that I heard a small child thanking You for many things. "And thank You for the lightning bugs," he said. What a simple reminder that there's nothing too insignificant for which to offer thanks.

....

....

....

....

....

....

....

....

....

....

....

....

....

CELEBRATE!

Start children off on the way they should go,
and even when they are old they
will not turn from it.

PROVERBS 22:6

One by one, the shower gifts circle the room. Guests paw through bibs and colorful toys and stroke velvet dresses and crocheted blankets. Diapers, in four different sizes, are stacked in the corner. The mother-to-be glows. We are her church family, gathered together to celebrate a new birth. We give gifts that will contribute to the child's now and the child's future. The best gift of all is a family who is no stranger to Your Word. Lord, keep this family walking in Your ways—now and in the future.

....

....

....

....

....

....

....

....

....

....

....

....

BELIEF

*He that cometh to God must believe that he is,
and that he is a rewarder of them
that diligently seek him.*
HEBREWS 11:6 KJV

Belief is one of those things that you can't see physically, but you still have it. For example, you believe a chair will hold you when you sit in it. You can't explain the physics of it, but you sit in it believing it will do what it's supposed to do. Belief in God is like that. You trust that He will do what He said He would do. The Bible, His written Word, is filled with those promises.

SHOUTS OF JOY

*"He will yet fill your mouth with laughter
and your lips with shouts of joy."*
Job 8:21

Do you remember the last time you laughed till you cried? For many of us, it's been far too long. Stress tends to steal our joy, leaving us humorless and oh so serious. But lightness and fun haven't disappeared forever. They may be buried beneath the snow of a long, wintry life season, but spring is coming, girls. Laughter will bloom again, and our hearts will soar as our lips shout with joy. Grasp that hope!

....

....

....

....

....

....

....

....

....

....

....

....

....

Day 47

INVESTED IN GOD

*Jesus said to her, "I am the resurrection and the life. The one who believes
in me will live, even though they die; and whoever lives by believing
in me will never die. Do you believe this?"*

JOHN 11:25–26

Your beliefs say a lot about your future. For example, believing that hard
work leads to success will help you meet your goals. Believing that true love
lasts forever will help you remain steadfast in your marriage. And believing
that God has promised you life everlasting will allow you to continue to value
yourself even as your body ages and your earthly life winds down. Beliefs
are important, and those invested in God pay the biggest dividends of all.

....

....

....

....

....

....

....

....

....

....

....

GOOD ANGER

*Be ye angry, and sin not: let not the
sun go down upon your wrath.*
EPHESIANS 4:26 KJV

We have valid reasons for anger when we see wrongdoing against the innocent. But God tells us not to let that anger last long. We need to come to Him in prayer, consider the issue in Him, and ultimately leave it in His hands. If we can help correct the wrong, we should. But letting ourselves dwell on the situation until we fume is not an option. Let anger push us to do good, not ruin our emotional health.

....

....

....

....

....

....

....

....

....

....

....

....

A WORD IN DUE SEASON

Everyone enjoys a fitting reply; it is wonderful
to say the right thing at the right time!
PROVERBS 15:23 NLT

Ever had a friend approach you at just the right time—say, when you were really down—and speak something positive and uplifting? Ah, what perfect timing! You needed to hear something good, something pleasant. The right word at the right time was just what the doctor ordered, causing joy to spring up in your soul. The next time you see a friend going through a rough time, decide to speak that "good word."

....

....

....

....

....

....

....

....

....

....

....

....

THINK AHEAD

*A prudent person foresees danger
and takes precautions.*
PROVERBS 22:3 NLT

Wisdom means planning for the worst, anticipating the best, and trusting God with every outcome. Whether you're researching colleges, purchasing a home, getting married, having a baby, starting a new company, or taking care of your aging parents, you'll want to ask intelligent questions and plan for your next steps. God encourages you to think ahead. Seek the advice of trusted friends and associates, take necessary precautions, and then turn the results over to Him.

Day 51

ENCOURAGING OTHERS

*And we know that all things work together for
good to them that love God, to them who are
the called according to his purpose.*

ROMANS 8:28 KJV

You gave me an amazing opportunity today, Father, and it's all the result of a discouraging situation. You helped me as I struggled through the problem, and because of that I was able to encourage someone else who faced a similar difficulty. You really are an awesome God!

SIGHT UNSEEN

*The hope of eternal life, which God, who does
not lie, promised before the beginning of time.*
TITUS 1:2

The wedding ring has no beginning and no end. It is often used as an analogy of the unending love between a bride and groom. With a wedding ring, a spouse has agreed to a promise of commitment, but too often there is an end. God promised us eternal life before the beginning of time. He gave us His Son to highlight the unending love between a father and child. He has never strayed from that promise.

....

....

....

....

....

....

....

....

....

....

....

GOD'S GIFT TO YOU

Children are a gift from the Lord;
they are a reward from him.
Psalm 127:3 nlt

If you're a mother, you know how precious your children are to you. They are bone of your bone, flesh of your flesh. You would not hesitate to protect them with your life. And well you should, for that's your job. Take a moment to remember that you are God's child, created in His own image. He gave His very life to save you, and even now He hovers over you protectively. Your children are God's gift to you. You are God's gift to Himself.

DANCING IN THE PUDDLES

And so, Lord, where do I put my hope?
My only hope is in you.
PSALM 39:7 NLT

They say you can tell a lot about a person's foundation of hope by the way she handles a rainy day. Does she turn into a gloomy Gussy, wailing, "Oh, woe is me," or does she make the best of a bad situation? A hope-filled person will realize that abundant life in Christ isn't about simply enduring the storm but also about learning to dance in the puddles. So grab your galoshes, and let's boogie!

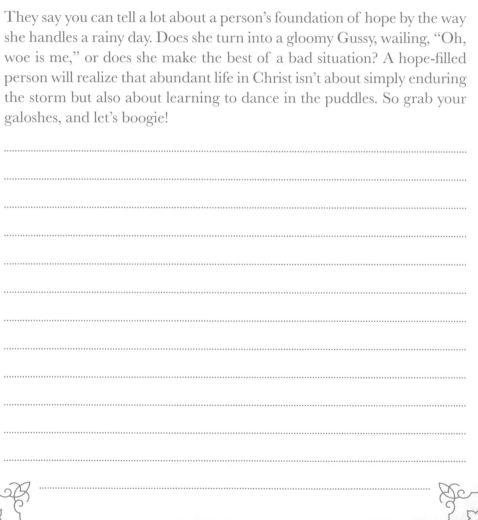

Day 55

DECEPTION

*Jesus answered, "I am the way, and the
truth, and the life. The only way
to the Father is through me."*
JOHN 14:6 NCV

If you've ever been deceived, you know how devastating it can be. Not only
do you feel hurt, but your sense of trust is shaken as well. Maybe that's why
God so often reminds us in the Bible that He represents truth, pure and
simple. There is no deception in Him. He won't try to secure your love with
empty promises. He can be trusted. Wrap your heart and mind around that
truth, and let it heal you.

....

....

....

....

....

....

....

....

....

....

....

Day 56

TODAY!

*"Therefore do not worry about tomorrow,
for tomorrow will worry about itself.
Each day has enough trouble of its own."*

<small>MATTHEW 6:34</small>

You can look ahead and obsess about fears for the future or take life one day at a time and enjoy it. But you live only in today, not in the weeks, months, and years that may lie ahead. You can change life only in the moment you're in now. Since worry never improves the future and only hurts today, you'll benefit most from trusting in God and enjoying the spot where He has planted you for now.

RIGHTEOUSNESS, PEACE, AND JOY

*For the kingdom of God is not meat
and drink; but righteousness, and peace,
and joy in the Holy Ghost.*
ROMANS 14:17 KJV

Sometimes life can be a drudgery. We wake up in the morning, get dressed, and go to work (or stay home to care for our children). We drag ourselves home in the evening, spend a little time with our loved ones, then drop into bed, exhausted. There's so much more to life! The Lord wants to remind you that He has given you righteousness, peace, and joy—for every day of your life! So celebrate!

GLORIOUS!

The glory of the young is their strength;
the gray hair of experience is the splendor of the old.
PROVERBS 20:29 NLT

The expression "generation gap" became popular in the 1960s, although it probably existed in some uncoined sense throughout history. Young people don't *get* their grandparents, and the over-fifty crowd can't *figure out* their juniors—in some sense a standoff. But the truth is, there is beauty on both sides of the gap. Young people possess stamina and a passion for life, while those who've been around a while are reservoirs of experience and wisdom. In God we are glorious at any age.

THE CENTER OF GOD'S WILL

For God is working in you, giving you the desire
and the power to do what pleases him.
PHILIPPIANS 2:13 NLT

Lord, I know that in the center of Your will are peace, joy, and many other rich blessings. I'd like to experience all these things, but I seem to have trouble figuring out what Your will is for me. Please help me be attentive when You speak, and give me a heart willing to be used by You.

....

....

....

....

....

....

....

....

....

....

....

....

....

....

FALLEN

*"But blessed is the one who trusts in the L*ORD*, whose confidence is in him. They will be like a tree planted by the water that sends out its roots by the stream. It does not fear when heat comes; its leaves are always green. It has no worries in a year of drought and never fails to bear fruit."*

JEREMIAH 17:7–8

The tree looked sturdy and strong, yet torrential rains brought down a limb, and now the once proud oak appears flawed. When people pass the tree, they see only the broken branch and not the rest. What remains is still sturdy and strong. Lord, that downed branch is like the shedding of sin. Take it away so we no longer carry the burden. Help the world know us not for our weaknesses, but for the strengths we owe to You.

Day 61

BE AN EXAMPLE

*Be an example to the believers with your words,
your actions, your love, your faith,
and your pure life.*
1 TIMOTHY 4:12 NCV

Setting an example for others—always having to watch your words and your actions—can seem like a heavy weight. Being good on your own is an impossibility. There's only one way you can live worthy to represent God. That is by letting Him live through you. When your self-interest crowds to the forefront, surrender yourself to Him. Soon you will find yourself demonstrating for others that it is possible to live a pure and godly life.

....

....

....

....

....

....

....

....

....

....

....

....

Day 62

MY REFUGE

God is our refuge and strength,
always ready to help in times of trouble.
PSALM 46:1 NLT

What is your quiet place—the place you go to get away from the fray, to chill out, think, regroup, and gain perspective? Mine is a hammock nestled beneath a canopy of oaks in my backyard—nobody around but birds, squirrels, an occasional wasp, God, and me. There I can pour out my heart to my Lord, hear His comforting voice, and feel His strength refresh me. We all need a quiet place. God, our refuge, will meet us there.

....

....

....

....

....

....

....

....

....

....

....

....

INSIDE AND OUT

Why, my soul, are you downcast? Why so disturbed within me?
Put your hope in God, for I will yet praise him, my Savior and my God.
PSALM 42:5

Depression is often a physiological problem, but just as often it's a result of adverse circumstances. If events in your life have left you in the depths of despair, God wants you to know that you are not alone. He is right there with you. Even when others don't understand, He does. Others see only who you are on the outside, but He knows all about you, inside and out. He knows how to comfort you. Reach out to Him, and He will reach back.

LIVING FOR CHRIST

If you live according to the flesh, you will die;
but if by the Spirit you put to death the
misdeeds of the body, you will live.
ROMANS 8:13

Living for Christ through His Spirit offers real life, overflowing and abundant. Blessings spill over in obedient lives. But the world, at war with God, doesn't understand. Unbelievers never feel the touch of the Spirit in their hearts and lives, and Jesus' gentle love is foreign to them. Put to death worldly misdeeds, and instead of the emptiness of the world, you'll receive blessings indeed.

THE NEW MAN

*And have put on the new self, which is being
renewed in knowledge in the image of its Creator.*
COLOSSIANS 3:10

Are there people in your life you've given up on? Maybe someone you've been praying for, for years? You're convinced he or she will never come to the Lord? Today ponder the new beginnings in your own life. Hasn't God recreated you? Renewed you? Won't He do the same for others? Feel the joy rise up as you ponder the possibilities. Pray for that friend or loved one to "put on the new self."

HE'S ANSWERING

*The LORD directs our steps, so why try to
understand everything along the way?*
PROVERBS 20:24 NLT

Are you tired of trying so hard to make sure you do everything just right?
Do you long to hear God whispering that He's with you and in control?
Then you're like many other busy and overworked women. God knows
your desire to love others, serve, and make wise choices. He hears your
genuine prayer for help and strength. And He's answering. So lean back
and take a deep breath. You are loved more than you'll ever know.

FAMILY BLESSINGS

*When you do things, do not let selfishness or pride
be your guide. Instead, be humble and give
more honor to others than to yourselves.*
PHILIPPIANS 2:3 NCV

Among Your many blessings, my family ranks near the top. They share my joys and help bear my burdens. Jesus, I know that You selected each of my relatives to be a part of my life in a special way, and I thank You for each of them. May I bring happiness to them in some way too!

Day 68

HE KNOWS MY NAME

"You have kept your promise to your servant David my father; with your mouth you have promised and with your hand you have fulfilled it—as it is today."
1 Kings 8:24

There are plaques that change the words of John 3:16 from "For God so loved the world. . ." to "For God so loved [insert your name here]. . ." Just as God spoke to David, just as God knew David personally, so He knows each one of us and keeps His promises to us.

....

....

....

....

....

....

....

....

....

....

....

....

....

A DAZZLING FUTURE

Good people can look forward to a bright future.
PROVERBS 13:9 NCV

When your life is hidden in the goodness of God, your possibilities are limitless. Your future is more than bright—it's dazzling. If you are at the beginning of your walk with God, you are a fortunate woman. The road ahead may not be easy, but it will be the greatest adventure, the greatest race you've ever attempted. And best of all, the destination is certain. Throw yourself unreservedly into the work that God has called you to. Take hold of your future with both hands.

SUPERWOMAN ISN'T HOME

*"But we will devote ourselves to prayer
and to the ministry of the word."*
ACTS 6:4 NASB

As busy women we've found out the hard way that we can't do everything. Heaven knows we've tried, but the truth has found us out: Superwoman is a myth. So we must make priorities and focus on what is most important. Prayer and God's Word should be our faith priorities. If we do as much as we can do, then God will take over and do what only He can do. He's got our backs, girls!

....

....

....

....

....

....

....

....

....

....

....

....

....

....

....

....

....

....

Day 71

DETERMINATION

*"Be strong and do not give up,
for your work will be rewarded."*

2 CHRONICLES 15:7

Have you ever watched a marathon? They can be pretty boring until the runners get to the final few miles. Some are so exhausted they can barely stay on their feet. You want to scream, "Give it up! It's just a race!" but they don't give up. The runners are determined to finish. They understand the reward that awaits them on the other side of the finish line, so they keep pushing. That's the kind of determination it takes to please God.

BLESSING OF FORGIVENESS

Your sins have been forgiven on account of his name.
1 JOHN 2:12

Who could do something wonderful enough to earn God's forgiveness? No human work can buy it. God forgives because of who He is, not because of who we are or what we do. That's encouraging, because we can't earn forgiveness by our own perfection. Instead, forgiveness becomes the great blessing of our Christian life that makes living for Jesus possible. We obey God to show our appreciation, not to gain entry into His kingdom.

SHOW YOURSELF FRIENDLY

*A man that hath friends must shew himself
friendly: and there is a friend that
sticketh closer than a brother.*
PROVERBS 18:24 KJV

Ever met someone who just seems to have the gift of friendship? She's a joy to be around and is always there when you need her. Perhaps you're that kind of friend to others. Friendship is a privilege, and we're blessed to have brothers and sisters in Christ. But not all friendships are easy. Today ask the Lord to show you how to "show yourself friendly" in every situation. Oh the joy of great relationships!

SHOW AND TELL

A refusal to correct is a refusal to love;
love your children by disciplining them.
PROVERBS 13:24 MSG

You want your children to make wise choices. You send them to the best school you can afford. You take them to church. You expect their teachers to instruct them well. And as their mother, you have the personal privilege of sharing what you've learned about living a God-honoring life. You show how much you love your children when you graciously tell *and* show them what is right and wrong in God's sight.

....

....

....

....

....

....

....

....

....

....

....

....

....

Day 75

MANAGING MONEY

*Therefore I say unto you, Take no thought for your life, what ye shall eat,
or what ye shall drink; nor yet for your body, what ye shall put on.
Is not the life more than meat, and the body than raiment?*
MATTHEW 6:25 KJV

It's funny, Lord. It seems like I always wish I had more money, but dealing with it can sometimes be a pain. Keeping it organized, making sure my bills are paid—at times it's overwhelming. Please give me a clear mind and wisdom to handle my financial responsibilities according to Your will.

....
....
....
....
....
....
....
....
....
....
....
....

NEWS TO ME

"We tell you the good news: What God promised our ancestors he has fulfilled for us, their children, by raising up Jesus."
ACTS 13:32–33

They say, "No news is good news." For the most part, I do not believe this is true. Now that I am a wife and mother, when the day grows dim and one of my loved ones is not where he should be, no news is scary and frustrating. Lord, You've kept nothing from us. You don't make us wait and worry. We know all Your news. And if we heed the message, nothing is scary or frustrating. We have Jesus to lead the way, to hold our hand. Thank You, Father, for the good news of Your promises and their endurance.

STRONG AND GENTLE

Let your gentleness be evident to all.
The Lord is near.

PHILIPPIANS 4:5

The Bible says that the strong woman is also gentle—two words that might seem contradictory. But they aren't. The strong woman chooses how she will respond to others. She chooses to deal with them gently—because she can. She is in control of her emotions, her words, and her actions. Anger, hostility—both represent the easy way out. But gentleness requires strength. God wants to see you become a strong, gentle woman for Him.

....

....

....

....

....

....

....

....

....

....

....

Day 78

TIME-OUT

"The Lord will not abandon His people."
1 Samuel 12:22 NASB

Do you remember when, as a little girl, you languished alone in your room as punishment? Or maybe you sat with your nose plastered to the corner in time-out. It felt as if your parents had abandoned you, didn't it? As adults we sometimes feel abandoned when that's not the case at all. We're actually in a place strategically chosen by a loving Father to teach us, broaden us, and improve us in the end.

_____

_____

_____

_____

_____

_____

_____

_____

_____

_____

_____

_____

_____

CREATED TO BE. . .

It was not with perishable things such as silver or gold that you were redeemed
from the empty way of life handed down to you from your ancestors,
but with the precious blood of Christ, a lamb without blemish or defect.

1 PETER 1:18–19

A deep feeling of emptiness drives many to addiction, despair, and risky behavior. Without a sense of meaning and purpose in their lives, who could blame them? Maybe you find yourself in that very place—empty through and through but you don't have to live that way. God loves you, and He has a purpose and plan for your life—a plan that will challenge you and bring you joy and fulfillment. Let Him fill you with His Holy Spirit and show you who you were created to be.

CHOSEN FAMILY

*There is a friend that sticketh
closer than a brother.*
PROVERBS 18:24 KJV

Family relationships range from the wonderful to the disturbing, and we get whatever God gives us. But we choose our friends based on common interests and experiences. Often this "chosen family" seems closer to us than siblings. Yet neither clings closer than our elder brother Jesus. He teaches us how to love blood relatives and those we choose. No matter whether we're related, when we love in Him, that love sticks fast.

GREETING ONE ANOTHER IN JOY

[Speak] to one another with psalms, hymns,
and songs from the Spirit. Sing and make
music from your heart to the Lord.

EPHESIANS 5:19

Want to try a fun experiment? The next time someone asks you how you're doing, instead of responding, "Okay," why not get more specific? Try "I'm blessed!" or "Having an awesome day!" Encourage yourself in the Lord, and He will keep those spirits lifted. And encourage one another with words of blessing as well.

....

....

....

....

....

....

....

....

....

....

....

....

....

....

A RELIABLE SOURCE

Without good direction, people lose their way; the more
wise counsel you follow, the better your chances.
Proverbs 11:14 msg

Have you ever thought you knew the way to an appointment destination only to discover you were driving in the opposite direction? Frustrating, isn't it? Asking a reliable source for directions to follow greatly reduces your chances of ending up at an unwanted destination. Likewise, it's a sensible idea to pause and seek help when you feel lost in a relationship, with your job, or in your spiritual life. Following wise counsel enhances your chances for fulfillment, success, and growth.

A FRIEND'S FORGIVENESS

For if ye forgive men their trespasses,
your heavenly Father will also forgive you.
MATTHEW 6:14 KJV

I can't believe it, Father. I really messed up this time, and my friend still forgave me. I didn't really expect her ever to want to speak to me again, but she hugged me and told me we'd just start again. That felt so wonderful! Thank You for friends who forgive.

WHERE ARE YOU?

But if from there you seek the LORD your God,
you will find him if you seek him with
all your heart and with all your soul.

DEUTERONOMY 4:29

One day the rearview mirror separated from the windshield of my car. For the first few moments, the loss didn't bother me. For the next few weeks—the time it took me to replace the mirror—every time I went to check my mirror, I was bothered. You see, habit kept me looking for the mirror. As a driver I was impaired. Lord, in so many ways, You are like that mirror. You stand beside us, and sometimes we do not even realize You are there, but should we lose sight of You, we are bothered; we are impaired. Lord, always keep us faithfully looking at You.

....

....

....

....

....

....

....

....

....

....

"GOD-NESS"

*As we have opportunity, let us do good to all people,
especially to those who belong to the family of believers.*
GALATIANS 6:10

Good deeds are an expression of the goodness or "God-ness" that resides within you. They should come easily, naturally. As you feel God's presence within and see Him moving in your affairs, as you feel your heart flooding with gratitude for what He has done for you, reach out to others. Let them feel the overflow of God's goodness to you. Good deeds aren't something you force yourself to do. They are the joyous privilege of the child of God.

....

....

....

....

....

....

....

....

....

....

....

....

....

....

....

....

....

BIGGER AND BETTER

Waiting does not diminish us, any more than waiting diminishes a pregnant mother. . . . The longer we wait. . .the more joyful our expectancy.
ROMANS 8:24–25 MSG

Life is filled with waiting—on slow people, on transportation, on doctor's reports, even for God to act. Waiting often requires patience we don't have. It feels like perpetual pregnancy—anticipating a baby that is never delivered. The secret is to clasp hands with our Lord. He offers His shield of protection from impatience, irritability, and anger and replaces them with self-control, kindness, and joy. Waiting is inevitable, but we can draw closer to the Father in the waiting.

YOUR BEST

Whatever work you do, do your best.
ECCLESIASTES 9:10 NCV

By necessity, many people work in jobs they don't like or feel suited for. For them, work is a duty rather than a dream. If you find yourself in that situation, there is something you can do. Take one day at a time, and focus your attention on your responsibilities for that day. Give it your all as a token of your love and respect for God. You will either begin to see your job differently, or God will find you a new assignment. He always rewards the diligent.

LOVING JESUS

*Looking unto Jesus the author
and finisher of our faith. . .*
HEBREWS 12:2 KJV

God is writing a story of faith through your life. What will it describe? Will it be a chronicle of challenges overcome, like the Old Testament story of Joseph? Or a near tragedy turned into joy, like that of the prodigal son? Whatever your account says, if you love Jesus, the end is never in question. Those who love Him finish in heaven, despite their trials on earth. The long, weary path ends in His arms. Today write a chapter in your faithful narrative of God's love.

....

....

....

....

....

....

....

....

....

....

....

Day 89

JOY IN PLACE OF TEARS

They that sow in tears shall reap in joy.
PSALM 126:5 KJV

Periods of great sorrow are unavoidable. Perhaps the death of a loved one has left you floundering. Or maybe your heart has been broken by someone you thought you could trust. If you've been through an earth-shaking change—one you weren't expecting or feel you didn't deserve—then turn to the One who can replenish you. God will walk with you through this valley and promises to replace your tears with joy.

....

....

....

....

....

....

....

....

....

....

....

....

....

....

....

....

A PROTECTIVE HEDGE

Discretion will preserve you;
understanding will keep you.

PROVERBS 2:11 NKJV

Sometimes when a farmer wants to protect his territory, he plants a thorny hedge around the perimeter. He hopes it will protect his land and possessions from harm. Discretion—or the ability to meditate, think, purpose, and plan—works like a protective hedge in your life. Not only does God provide you with wisdom and instruction for making wise decisions, but He helps you gain the resources and knowledge needed for reasoning, organizing, and implementing your future plans.

LORD, CARRY MY FRIEND

As for me, since I am poor and needy, let the Lord keep me in his thoughts.
You are my helper and my savior. O my God, do not delay.
PSALM 40:17 NLT

My friend is hurting, dear Jesus. She's had so many struggles in her life lately, and she feels as if she's about to hit rock bottom. I've tried to be there for her, but right now she needs You in a special way. Please let her know that You want to carry her through this trial. Help her to trust You.

FATHER'S DAY

*"I am the good shepherd; I know my
sheep and my sheep know me."*
JOHN 10:14

The moon spills its light over the baseball diamond, and the silhouettes of a father and child can be seen traipsing across the pitcher's mound. The father takes confident strides. The toddler bebops about eight feet behind. As if a magnet were holding him in place, the toddler seldom strays from following his father's footsteps, and when he does stray, the father stops, turns, and puts him back on the right course. Jesus, You are like that father. You lead, and I follow, and should I stray, You want to guide me back on course.

RESULTS

"I will refresh the weary and satisfy the faint."
JEREMIAH 31:25

Satisfaction is the result of a job well done. Sometimes your expectation for the blessings of God requires you to press a little harder and stretch your faith a little further to see the results you've asked God for. You can be sure all your effort will be rewarded. God promises to satisfy your soul—a deep satisfaction only He can provide. He has given you the power to reach your destiny. He will not let you fail. Press on! Press on!

....
....
....
....
....
....
....
....
....
....
....
....
....

CLIMB IN

May the God of hope fill you with all joy and peace as you trust in him,
so that you may overflow with hope by the power of the Holy Spirit.

ROMANS 15:13

Trust is the bottom line when it comes to living an abundant life. We will never escape the muddy ruts without trusting that God has the leverage and power to pull us out of the quagmire. They say faith is like believing the tightrope walker can cross the gorge pushing a wheelbarrow. Only when we trust God and climb into His wheelbarrow can His joy and peace overflow as hope into our hearts.

....

....

....

....

....

....

....

....

....

....

....

....

A POSITIVE MESSAGE

My comfort in my suffering is this:
Your promise preserves my life.
PSALM 119:50

Things like divorce can leave lifelong consequences in their wake, even affecting and infecting future relationships. Though you may be facing some of the negative results of divorce, God offers a positive message: He forgives you, regardless of what you may have said and done. And He comforts you with His unchanging promise of everlasting love and eternal life. Just ask Him, and He'll tell you as many times as you need to hear it.

BE PREPARED

He has also set eternity in the human heart;
yet no one can fathom what God has
done from beginning to end.
ECCLESIASTES 3:11

Though each of us has a bit of eternity in her heart, and we cannot rest unless we know the Savior, we also cannot fathom the works of God. That can either make us dissatisfied and doubtful or relaxed, trusting children who know their Father is in control and will care for them from beginning to end. Have you trusted Him who is the Alpha and Omega? Are you prepared for eternity with Him?

....

....

....

....

....

....

....

....

....

....

....

....

JOY IN THE FAMILY

*Now the God of hope fill you with all joy
and peace in believing, that ye may abound in
hope, through the power of the Holy Ghost.*

ROMANS 15:13 KJV

Living in a family environment isn't always easy. Siblings bicker. Tempers flare. People get their feelings hurt. If you want to experience joy in your family, then ask the Lord to give you hope, especially when things are going wrong. Through the power of the Holy Spirit, you can overcome those obstacles, but you have to address them head-on. Today make a list of problems you're facing; then ask for God's input.

RELEASE

Trust GOD from the bottom of your heart;
don't try to figure out everything on your own.
PROVERBS 3:5 MSG

Doubts come. They're part of your human nature. God knows that. Things have happened to you that make trusting Him seem foolish. It can feel like the ultimate paradox to release what you've worked so hard to cultivate. Yet God loves you and wants to ease your fear and anxiety. Picture unclenching the fist of your heart and releasing the problems you've tried relentlessly to figure out on your own. You don't have to do life alone. God waits patiently.

....

....

....

....

....

....

....

....

....

....

....

....

....

TO-DO LISTS

Why am I discouraged? Why is my heart so sad?
I will put my hope in God! I will praise
him again—my Savior and my God!
PSALM 42:11 NLT

I didn't really think my goals were far-fetched. My to-do list had only three major tasks, yet I barely made it through two. It seems I've worked all day and accomplished nothing. I feel disgusted with myself, but tomorrow's another day, Lord. Give me the right attitude as I begin again.

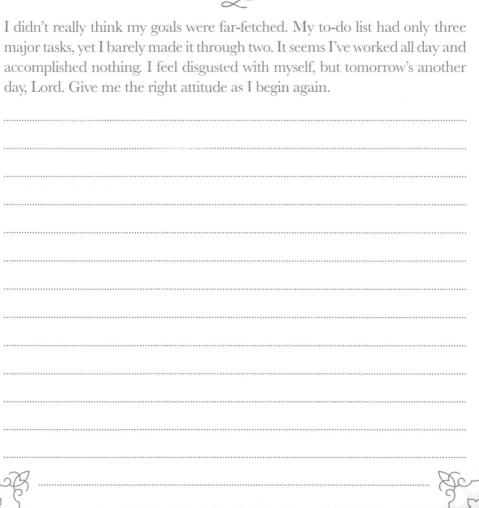

ULTIMATE CARING

Children's children are a crown to the aged,
and parents are the pride of their children.
PROVERBS 17:6

If I could go back in time and change just one thing, it would be this: my appreciation of my parents. Too late I realized the precious gift of their unwavering love. Too late I realized the dedication they gave to guiding me in the paths of righteousness. Too late I realized that in the whole wide world, no one loves like a caring parent. And, Father, I do realize that You are the ultimate caring Parent.

GIFT OF SELF-CONTROL

*With minds that are alert and fully sober,
set your hope on the grace to be brought to you
when Jesus Christ is revealed at his coming.*
1 PETER 1:13

There are moments in every woman's life when her emotions take on a life of their own. When those times come to your life, God wants you to walk by faith and not by sight—being led by confidence in Him rather than your feelings. The gift of self-control will put you in His best light and keep you from responding foolishly. He stands ready to help you choose self-control. Believe in Him because He believes in you.

SMALL BUT MIGHTY

"He has. . .exalted the humble."
LUKE 1:52 NLT

God delights in making small things great. He's in the business of taking scrap-heap people and turning them into treasures: Noah (the laughingstock of his city), Moses (stuttering shepherd turned national leader), David (smallest among the big and powerful), Sarah (old and childless), Mary (poor teenager), Rahab (harlot turned faith-filled ancestor of Jesus). So you and I can rejoice with hope! Let us glory in our smallness!

MORE LIKE CHRIST

Bear with each other and forgive one another if any of you has a grievance against someone. Forgive as the Lord forgave you. And over all these virtues put on love, which binds them all together in perfect unity.
COLOSSIANS 3:13–14

No family is perfect, and nearly everyone will at some time hurt, betray, and disappoint a family member. In extreme cases, it may be necessary to distance yourself. But in all cases, it is necessary to forgive. Let God judge the person or people who caused the pain. To you He says, "Forgive." When you do, you will no longer harm yourself with the corrosive emotions of anger and resentment. Instead, you will become more like Christ, who long ago forgave you.

HOLD ON TO HOPE

The prospect of the righteous is joy,
but the hopes of the wicked come to nothing.
PROVERBS 10:28

Trusting in Jesus gave you new life and hope for eternity. So how do you respond when life becomes dark and dull? Does hope slip away? When no obviously great spiritual works are going on, do not assume that God has deserted you. Hold on to Him even more firmly and trust. He will keep His promises. Truly, what other option do you have? Without Him hope disappears.

JOYOUS PERSPECTIVE

Let us draw near to God with a sincere heart
and with the full assurance that faith brings.

HEBREWS 10:22

Ever looked through a pair of binoculars? What if you peered through the lenses and caught a glimpse of God's face? What if you could see things the way He sees them? Hear things the way He hears them? What an amazing perspective! Every time you draw near to God, He offers you the opportunity to see Him, to find Him, to trust Him. Let Him give you His joyous perspective today.

A WARM, SAFE PLACE

*The integrity of good people
creates a safe place for living.*
PROVERBS 14:32 MSG

Whatever your role—sister, aunt, mother, daughter, spouse—you enjoy sharing good times with those you love. You also want them to feel comfortable approaching you with their disappointments. But how? A wise woman knows that others feel safe with someone who is the same on the inside as she is on the outside—one who listens first and then talks. Ask God to help you create a warm and safe place for your family to live and share.

BAD HAPPINESS

*Repent therefore of this thy wickedness,
and pray God, if perhaps the thought of
thine heart may be forgiven thee.*
ACTS 8:22 KJV

I'm embarrassed, Lord, and I need Your cleansing. Someone at church has been giving me trouble for a while. I just discovered that something unfortunate happened to him, and I gloated. I tried to keep my happiness undercover, but it was there, and it shouldn't have been. Please don't let me rejoice at others' misfortunes.

CALORIE COUNT

*Out of his fullness we have all received
grace in place of grace already given.*
JOHN 1:16

Why can't celery taste like brownies? I would never battle weight again if brownies had the same calorie count as celery! Lord, sometimes the things we so desire are the things that You warn us against. And, in the end, should we partake, we experience the repercussions. It will take me a good year to shed the brownies that hug my hips. I thank You that I can more easily shed sin by Your grace.

....
....
....
....
....
....
....
....
....
....
....
....
....

RAINING DOWN

Rejoice in the LORD your God, for he has given you the autumn rains because he is faithful. He sends you abundant showers, both autumn and spring rains.

JOEL 2:23

As human beings we are limited in what we can provide for those we love—our resources, both material and emotional, are finite. But God has no limits. He blesses His children far beyond our comprehension. He does more than just rain down His blessings on us; He sends abundant showers of blessing in every season of our lives. You are a rich woman. Once you see all that God has provided for you, you won't ever want to come in out of the rain.

....

....

....

....

....

....

....

....

....

....

....

....

....

....

....

....

HIT THE MATS

Blessed are those whose help is the God of Jacob,
whose hope is in the LORD their God.

PSALM 146:5

Wrestled with God lately? We all do at one time or another. The Genesis 32 account of Jacob's almighty wrestling match reassures us that God is not offended when we beat on His chest and shout, "Why?" He understands that we must sometimes wrestle out the mysteries of our faith. Wrestling with his Lord was a turning point for Jacob—he got a new name (Israel) and a new perspective. God is ready to do the same for us.

....

....

....

....

....

....

....

....

....

....

....

IN NEED OF FREEDOM?

The LORD sets prisoners free.
PSALM 146:7

We take for granted the ability to move about at will, make independent choices, and manage our own affairs. Many in this world are not so fortunate. They are prisoners. Some are being held in prison for illegal acts; others live in nations where they are prisoners by the will of the government. Still others are prisoners of their own behaviors and excesses. To all the prisoners, God offers the freedom to receive His love and grace, the freedom to know Him and serve Him. Are you in need of freedom?

....

....

....

....

....

....

....

....

....

....

....

....

....

....

BLESSING OTHERS

We work hard with our own hands. When we are cursed,
we bless; when we are persecuted, we endure it.

1 CORINTHIANS 4:12

God gave Paul many blessings, and the apostle passed them on, even if the recipients didn't seem to really deserve them. Those who cursed him (and they were, no doubt, many) did not receive cursing in return. Instead, Paul tried to bless them. Do we follow the apostle's example? When we are cursed by the words of others, what is our response?

....

....

....

....

....

....

....

....

....

....

....

....

Day 113

"HAPPY IS HE (OR SHE!). . ."

Where there is no vision, the people perish:
but he that keepeth the law, happy is he.
PROVERBS 29:18 KJV

Ever wish you could see into tomorrow? Wish you knew what was coming around the bend? While we can't see into the future, we can prepare for it by trusting God to bring us His very best. And while our "literal" vision can't glimpse the unseen tomorrow, we can prepare for it by staying close to the Lord and spending time in His Word. Peace and joy come when we trust God with our future.

DIVERSE FRIENDSHIPS

Whoever walks with the wise becomes wise.
PROVERBS 13:20 NRSV

Isn't it amazing how diverse friendships can be? You may have friends for different seasons of your life or friends with whom you share a particular interest, friends you've had forever, and friends you've just met. It's essential, though, that you include those who are wise in your circle of friends. Spending time with people who have sound judgment will help you stay clearheaded and moving in the direction of a blessing-filled life.

CHRIST STILL HEALS

The LORD protects all those who love him,
but he destroys the wicked.
PSALM 145:20 NLT

You brought healing to so many people in the Bible, Jesus. Those were exciting times for those individuals, and it's still a spectacular miracle when You make someone whole today. Thank You for the many times You've touched my sick body or brought relief to my loved ones. Your loving touch produces great joy.

....

....

....

....

....

....

....

....

....

....

....

....

....

....

....

....

Day 116

HOT TO COLD

Have mercy on me, O God, according to your unfailing love;
according to your great compassion blot out my transgressions.
Wash away all my iniquity and cleanse me from my sin.
PSALM 51:1–2

I run my hand underneath the water and adjust the temperature. Right now it's running cool. I turn up the hot water. Ah, just right. Then I step in and yelp. Too hot! Lord, sometimes sin tempts us by appearing harmless, but like water temperature that can change in a moment's time, so can our involvement in sin. Water burns; sin does too, but its scars run deeper. Guide our steps, Lord, and forgive and cleanse us from our sins.

PEACEFUL SLEEP

*In peace I will lie down and sleep,
for you alone, LORD, make me dwell in safety.*

PSALM 4:8

Strangely, your body was designed like a battery. It runs down and has to be recharged. That's why sleep is so important. Your body powers down and reaches a point in which you are fully relaxed. Then you begin to refuel and rebuild. It's a time of restoration for your body and your mind. The Lord has promised you the blessing of peaceful sleep. You can relax and take comfort, knowing He never sleeps but watches over you at all times.

GO FOR IT

When everything was hopeless,
Abraham believed anyway, deciding to
live. . .on what God said he would do.
ROMANS 4:18 MSG

"You can't do that. It's impossible." Have you ever been told this? Or just thought it because of fear or a previous experience with failure? This world is full of those who discourage rather than encourage. If we believe them, we'll never do anything. But if we, like Abraham, believe that God has called us for a particular purpose, we'll press toward that goal despite our track records. Past failure doesn't dictate future failure. If God wills it, He fulfills it.

....

....

....

....

....

....

....

....

....

....

....

....

....

HEAVENLY FATHER

The mighty God, The everlasting Father. . .
Isaiah 9:6 kjv

If you have accepted Jesus as your Savior, God is always your Father. Distance, disagreement, or death cannot change that, though each may separate you from your earthly father. But a human parent is neither mighty nor everlasting and may fail physically or spiritually. Only your heavenly Father will always be there for you, guiding you every step of the way. When you need help, call on your Father; He will never fail.

SEEK OUT WISDOM

I applied mine heart to know, and to search,
and to seek out wisdom.
ECCLESIASTES 7:25 KJV

Remember when you participated in your first Easter egg hunt? You searched under every bush, every tree until you found one of those shiny eggs. The quest for wisdom is much like that. You have to look under a lot of shrubs to find it, especially in this day and age. Oh, but what a prize! Today, as you apply your heart to the Word of God, seek out wisdom. What a joyous treasure!

....

....

....

....

....

....

....

....

....

....

....

....

....

Day 121

INFLUENCING OTHERS

Good leadership is a channel of water controlled by GOD;
he directs it to whatever ends he chooses.

PROVERBS 21:1 MSG

You are a leader. Maybe you don't think so, but you are. Someone looks up to you and would like your support, advice, and encouragement. Perhaps you doubt your ability to lead well. Still, you long to live and inspire others with a sincere heart—with intentionality, wisdom, and grace. Be encouraged, because God loves to guide you. Partner with him, and be assured that He's working in you to influence others for good.

....

....

....

....

....

....

....

....

....

....

....

....

....

WHERE THE HEART IS

But concerning brotherly love you have no need that I should write to you,
for you yourselves are taught by God to love one another.

1 THESSALONIANS 4:9 NKJV

I've heard it said that home is where the heart is, and I suppose there's a lot of truth in that. My home is such a special place, and it seems that often when I'm somewhere else, I am longing to be back in that place, surrounded by what is comfortable and familiar. Thank You, Lord, for that opportunity to return home.

....

....

....

....

....

....

....

....

....

....

....

....

....

....

....

....

....

....

THAT THING YOU DO

The LORD God is a sun and shield; the LORD bestows favor and honor;
no good thing does he withhold from those whose walk is blameless.
PSALM 84:11

Lord, You position Yourself between us and sin. Oh to be blameless, to always make the right choices. It's only through You that I can be blameless and forgiven. Lord, I recognize Your presence and ask Your forgiveness for all the times that I, like an errant child, didn't stay where I should.

OPEN YOUR HEART

Do not forget to do good and to share with others,
for with such sacrifices God is pleased.
HEBREWS 13:16

The true meaning of hospitality is opening up your heart to others, making them feel at home in your presence. That means you can be hospitable anywhere you are. It doesn't require a fancy house or a gourmet meal. When you reach out to someone else with love and acceptance, you have shown that person hospitality. Look around you. Ask God to show you those people whom you can minister to just by opening your heart.

....

....

....

....

....

....

....

....

....

....

....

....

....

REST STOP

*So let's not allow ourselves to get fatigued doing good. At the right
time we will harvest a good crop if we don't give up, or quit.*
GALATIANS 6:9 MSG

As women we're used to serving others. It's part of the feminine package.
But sometimes we get burned out. Fatigued. Overburdened. Girls, God
doesn't want us to be washed-out dishrags, to be so boggled that we try
to pay for groceries with our library card. It's up to us to recognize the
symptoms of burnout, and then rest, regroup, reenergize. This is not
indulgent; it's necessary to do our best in His name. So give yourself
permission to rest today.

PATIENT HEARTS

Patience is better than strength.
PROVERBS 16:32 NCV

"I'm not a patient person!" You've heard it said, and perhaps you've even said it yourself. Unfortunately, the statement supports a false idea about patience. Rather than an inborn personality trait given only to some, patience is a gift of the Holy Spirit worked in the hearts of those who love Him. Godly patience allows you to respond to life's trying situations with serenity and self-control, sure evidence of your continuing walk with God.

....

....

....

....

....

....

....

....

....

....

....

....

....

STAND FIRM

The LORD has become my fortress,
and my God the rock in whom I take refuge.
PSALM 94:22

Are you under attack by friends, family, or coworkers? If it comes because of your obedience to the Lord, stand firm in the face of their comments. He will defend you. If you face harsh words or nasty attitudes, remain kind, and He will assist you. Should your boss do you wrong, don't worry. Those who are against a faithful Christian are also against God, and He will somehow make things right.

THE KEY TO HAPPINESS

He who heeds the word wisely will find good,
and whoever trusts in the LORD, happy is he.

PROVERBS 16:20 NKJV

Want the key to true happiness? Try wisdom. When others around you are losing their heads, losing their cool, and losing sleep over their decisions, choose to react differently. Step up to the plate. Handle matters wisely. Wise choices always lead to joyous outcomes. And along the way, you will be setting an example for others around you to follow. So c'mon, get happy! Get wisdom!

....

....

....

....

....

....

....

....

....

....

....

....

LIBERATING OBEDIENCE

*Follow my advice. . .always treasure my commands. Obey my commands
and live! Guard my instructions as you guard your own eyes.*
PROVERBS 7:1–2 NLT

Obedience is not a popular word today. If you're like many adult women,
you don't want someone telling you what to do and who to be. You dread
being quashed by another's demands. Yet when God asks you to obey His
directives, He's liberating you. His guidelines help you take care of your
soul. Follow Him to become the best you can be.

....

....

....

....

....

....

....

....

....

....

....

....

....

....

....

....

YES, GOD LOVES ME

I am convinced that nothing can ever separate us from God's love.
Neither death nor life, neither angels nor demons, neither our fears for
today nor our worries about tomorrow—not even the powers
of hell can separate us from God's love.

ROMANS 8:38 NLT

I've been concentrating so much on my grief, Lord, that I'm afraid my perspective of You has become warped. I wonder why You allow bad things to happen, and sometimes I even question whether You really love me. I know the truth is that You are right there with me, wanting me to trust and love You more. Help me keep that in focus.

....

....

....

....

....

....

....

....

....

....

....

....

....

....

....

....

THE RÉSUMÉ

We have different gifts, according to the
grace given to each of us.
ROMANS 12:6

I keep looking for my place at church. Am I a greeter? A teacher? A card writer? The Bible says he who is last will be first. Our minister quotes this often, yet I consider him to be more important than I. He says that without the pew packers, he'd be nothing. Oh Lord, thank You for the opportunity to lead, the opportunity to follow, the opportunity to be involved in Your will.

POWERFUL KINDNESS

*When the kindness and love of God our Savior appeared, he saved us,
not because of righteous things we had done, but because of his mercy.*
TITUS 3:4–5

Do you find it easy to offer kindness to those you feel deserve it, but not to those who don't? That's a normal human response. But when you begin to understand the fullness of God's kindness to you personally, you're apt to see things in a different light. You weren't deserving or even grateful, and yet He was kind to you. He held nothing back. Being kind to those who don't deserve it is a powerful way to demonstrate your likeness to your heavenly Father.

GOING THE DISTANCE

[David]. . .chose five smooth stones from the stream. . .and,
with his sling in his hand, approached the Philistine.
1 SAMUEL 17:40

That little dude David had no intention of backing down from his fight until it was finished. Notice he picked up five rocks, not just one. He was prepared to go the distance against his giant. He fully expected God to make him victorious, but he knew it wouldn't be easy. So you've used your first rock against your giant. Maybe even your second. But don't give up. Keep reloading your slingshot and go the distance. Victory is sweet!

....

....

....

....

....

....

....

....

....

....

....

....

Day 134

THE NEW YOU

Who shall separate us from the love of Christ? Shall trouble or hardship or persecution or famine or nakedness or danger or sword? . . . No, in all these things we are more than conquerors through him who loved us.
ROMANS 8:35, 37

As the Holy Spirit immerses your soul in the sweetness of God's love, your attitude and behavior undergo noticeable changes. Now you're more discerning in your choices and more thoughtful about what you say and do. Some people, however, will clamor for the "old you" back, even resorting to name-calling and slander when you refuse. Don't let their persecution sway you, but call on God, whose strength and comfort are yours in all situations you face.

SAVING GRACE

My soul finds rest in God;
my salvation comes from him.
PSALM 62:1

At the moment you repented of your sins and asked Jesus to control your life, God saved you. But He didn't stop there. Each day of your life, He continues His saving work. He redirects you, protects you, and provides for your every need. In any trouble, rest in Him. He will not fail.

....
....
....
....
....
....
....
....
....
....
....
....
....
....

CHILDLIKE HOPE

*For You have been my hope, Sovereign LORD,
my confidence since my youth.*
PSALM 71:5

Remember how as a child you waited on pins and needles for Christmas to come? You hoped against hope you would get those toys you asked for. You knew in your knower that good things were coming. That same level of expectation can motivate you as an adult. Your Father wants you to trust Him with childlike faith. Put your trust in Him—and watch how He moves on your behalf.

PROSPERITY

Trusting the LORD leads to prosperity.
PROVERBS 28:25 NLT

A teacher asked her students for their definition of prosperity. Various responses were shouted across the classroom: *good fortune, success, money, wealth, riches, abundance, financial gain, profits*. Merriam-Webster defines the word *prosperity* as "the condition of being successful or thriving; especially: economic well-being." Wise King Solomon's definition of prosperity probably included *shalom*—peace, safety, well-being. When you trust God and follow His lead, you receive a personal sense of well-being. You can rest, live, and work in that truth.

UNNATURAL HUMILITY

They should be rich in good works and generous to those in need,
always being ready to share with others.
1 Timothy 6:18 nlt

We're by nature very proud, Jesus. Humility certainly doesn't come easily. But You are humble, and You are the example I am to follow regardless of what comes readily. Teach me to be more like You. Teach me to be a servant.

....

....

....

....

....

....

....

....

....

....

....

....

....

....

PLANT IT AND IT WILL GROW

*But the word of God continued
to spread and flourish.*
ACTS 12:24

Apple trees grow where apple trees probably shouldn't be. The owner of the cabin admits that for years she and her husband tossed cores in the dirt. Today two apple trees provide a surprise delicacy for the area's birds. Sometimes, Lord, Your Word falls like those long-ago apple seeds fell—on the ears of people who are where they shouldn't be. Isn't it wonderful when Christianity spreads where Christianity wasn't before?

....

....

....

....

....

....

....

....

....

....

....

....

A STUDENT

Let the wise listen and add to their learning.
PROVERBS 1:5

Being a Christian is all about being a student in the things of God. What a wonderful blessing! Each day you are charged with getting to know your heavenly Father better and becoming more like Him. That will sometimes be painful as you discard old thought patterns and behaviors in favor of new ones, but it will always be productive, transforming you into the person God created you to be. Stay close to Him, listen, and learn all you can.

....

....

....

....

....

....

....

....

....

....

....

....

....

....

BRICK BY BRICK

*So then faith cometh by hearing,
and hearing by the word of God.*
ROMANS 10:17 KJV

Words are powerful. They cut. They heal. They confirm. God uses His Word to help us, to mold us, to make us more like Him. Our faith is built from the bricks of God's Word. Brick by brick, we erect, strengthen, and fortify that faith. But only if we truly listen and hear the Word of God.

Day 142

DISCOVERY

I will praise the LORD, who counsels me;
even at night my heart instructs me.

PSALM 16:7

When you're faced with a decision, you have a wise counselor in God's Word. Open the Bible, because in it God has revealed His will and His guidelines for the lives of His people, a necessary foundation for any good decision. You also have a wise counselor in His Holy Spirit. Let Him teach you how to pray about the decision you need to make. When you do these things, you will discover His answer.

....

....

....

....

....

....

....

....

....

....

....

....

....

....

THE GLORY OF JESUS

God chose you as firstfruits to be saved. . . . He called you. . .
that you might share in the glory of our Lord Jesus Christ.
2 THESSALONIANS 2:13–14

Did you know you share Jesus' glory? Not because you are doing a wonderful job as a Christian, but simply because He decided to call you to Himself. God chose to share Himself with you and to make you like His Son. Daily He calls you to learn more of His magnificence as you faithfully follow Him. Isn't it wonderful to share just a bit of God's greatness?

BROUGHT FORTH WITH JOY

He brought forth his people with joy,
and his chosen with gladness.

PSALM 105:43 KJV

Have you ever been delivered out of a terrible situation? Lifted out of it unharmed? Were you stunned when it happened? Had you given up? God is in the deliverance business! And when He lifts us out of impossible situations, we are overwhelmed with joy—and we're surprised! Why do we doubt His goodness? The next time you're in a tough spot, expect to be "brought forth with joy."

Day 145

PURPOSE-FILLED LIFE

It's through me, Lady Wisdom, that your life deepens, and the years of your life ripen. Live wisely and wisdom will permeate your life.
Proverbs 9:11–12 msg

It's never too late to discover more about your giftedness and personality. No matter what your age or season of life, all your experiences (your family, education, jobs, talents, and disappointments) matter. They merge together to make you the unique person you are. God wants to use your story wisely for your fulfillment and His glory. Be intentional about seeking wisdom, and partner with God for a purpose-filled rest of your life.

J-O-Y

*Therefore be imitators of God as dear children. And walk in love,
as Christ also has loved us and given Himself for us, an offering
and a sacrifice to God for a sweet-smelling aroma.*

EPHESIANS 5:1–2 NKJV

Jesus. Others. You. What a simple yet profound definition of joy. And I'm beginning to see just how much this really works. I guess that's because when You are first in my life, everything else is properly prioritized. Although putting others before myself isn't always easy, it feels wonderful when I do it.

....

....

....

....

....

....

....

....

....

....

....

Day 147

A ROSE BY ANY OTHER NAME

*The life of mortals is like grass, they flourish like a flower of the field;
the wind blows over it and it is gone, and its place remembers it no more.
But from everlasting to everlasting the LORD's love is with those who
fear him, and his righteousness with their children's children.*

PSALM 103:15–17

A stranger handed my son a rose. In the back seat of my car, my eighteen-month-old played with it for a few seconds, ate a petal, and then tossed the flower on the floorboard, where it eventually turned into a broken stem and scattered pieces. Lord, when we try to live without You, we are broken and displaced just like the forlorn rose. Thank You for the opportunity to grow in Your Word.

PURIFYING TOOL

Let marriage be held in honor by all.
HEBREWS 13:4 NRSV

Since God placed the first man and woman in the Garden of Eden, He has endorsed and blessed marriage. Except for those who have been set apart—like the apostle Paul—for singleness, God uses marriage as a tool to purify us. Through it He teaches lessons on faithfulness, trust, love, humility, service, gentleness, and much more. It is His refining fire. All the more reason to set your heart to live and grow within the boundaries of this holy union.

....

....

....

....

....

....

....

....

....

....

....

....

A PERFECT FIT

The LORD is good to those whose hope is in him,
to the one who seeks him.

LAMENTATIONS 3:25

Seeking God is, for some, like a child groping in a dark room for the light switch. She knows it's there; she just can't seem to put her fingers on it. Some search for God all their lives, trying on various religions like pairs of shoes. This one pinches. That one chafes. But we must bypass religious fluff for the heart of the matter: Jesus. The only way to God is through faith in Christ (John 14:6). Suddenly, the shoe fits!

FULFILLMENT

A longing fulfilled is a tree of life.
PROVERBS 13:12

Your deepest longings and cherished dreams hold a special place in your heart, and they hold a special place in God's heart too. He cares what you care about. If you yearn for the fulfillment of your dreams and desires, bring them to the One who knows all about needs, desires, longings, yearnings— and miracles. Trust Him to draw from your dreams the pleasure of godly fulfillment and the satisfaction of true contentment.

....

....

....

....

....

....

....

....

....

....

....

LEAN ON JESUS

*"Therefore if the Son makes you free,
you shall be free indeed."*

JOHN 8:36 NKJV

Sometimes we don't feel freed from sin. Temptations draw us even though we love Jesus. So His words here can be both comforting and challenging. The Jews wanted to trust in their spiritual history, not God. That plan didn't work well for them, and it won't work for us either. We can't rely on history or our past deeds to put sin behind us. What will work? Leaning on Jesus every day, trusting Him to make us free indeed!

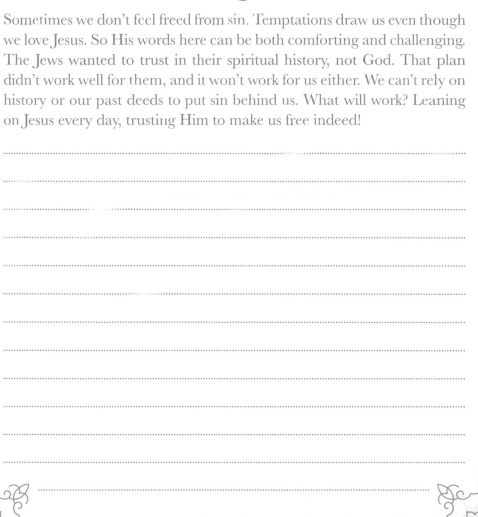

FINISHING WITH JOY

*But none of these things move me, neither count I my life dear
unto myself, so that I might finish my course with joy.*
ACTS 20:24 KJV

The Christian life is a journey, isn't it? We move from point A to point B, and then on from there—all the while growing in our faith. Instead of focusing on the ups and downs of the journey, we should be looking ahead to the finish line. We want to be people who finish well. Today set your sights on that unseen line that lies ahead. What joy will come when you cross it!

RELATIONSHIPS

As iron sharpens iron,
so a friend sharpens a friend.
Proverbs 27:17 NLT

Have you ever tried to cut a friend's hair with styling scissors that had dull blades? Or slice through a piece of steak with an unsharpened knife? It's frustrating, and the results are less than satisfying. Yet when you rub the dull blade against a separate piece of iron, it works better. Likewise, when you interact with a good friend, sharing honest feedback, encouraging each other's growth, you each become wiser. How rewarding is that?

....

....

....

....

....

....

....

....

....

....

....

....

JOYFUL KNOWLEDGE

Drink the Spirit of God, huge draughts of him. Sing hymns instead of drinking songs! Sing songs from your heart to Christ. Sing praises over everything, any excuse for a song to God the Father in the name of our Master, Jesus Christ.

EPHESIANS 5:19–20 MSG

Although the world might not think that my circumstances always warrant a song, I am rejoicing in the knowledge of what lies ahead. I have perfect hope of an eternity with You. I have joy in the belief that You are with me each step of the way. You have put a smile in my heart. Thank You, Lord.

....

....

....

....

....

....

....

....

....

....

....

....

....

BLESS THIS HOUSE

*"Honor your father and your mother, so that you may live
long in the land the LORD your God is giving you."*
EXODUS 20:12

A picture of my parents hangs above my desk. Both are smiling. They saw
to it that I was in church just about every time the door opened. They
held my hand; they gave me shelter; they gave me love. They were about
my age when the photo was taken. Now they wait for me in glory. They
were what God meant for a mother and father to be.

....

....

....

....

....

....

....

....

....

....

....

....

SPLENDID CREATION

God's glory is on tour in the skies,
God-craft on exhibit across the horizon.
PSALM 19:1 MSG

Look outside right now; better yet, go outside. Daytime or nighttime, it doesn't matter. Just look around you. If you live in a concrete jungle, look up at the sky. Imagine for a moment the immensity of God's creation, the grandeur of it. And yet He calls humankind His most splendid creation— all the rest was called into being only to benefit His human creation. God values you above all else. Look up at the sky and consider that.

REDEEMED!

*O Israel, hope in the L*ORD*; for with the L*ORD *there is lovingkindness,*
and with Him is abundant redemption.

PSALM 130:7 NASB

The psalmist knew Israel had a rotten track record. Throughout Old Testament history, God miraculously delivered the Israelites from trouble repeatedly, and they would gratefully turn to Him, only to eventually slip again into rebellion and more trouble. Sounds a lot like you and me, doesn't it? But thankfully, ours is a redemptive God, a God who offers abundant loving-kindness and forgiveness. A God of second chances—then and now.

GRACE IS YOURS

*How rich is God's grace, which he has
given to us so fully and freely.*
EPHESIANS 1:7–8 NCV

You may be having a difficult time accepting God's undeserved love.
Instead, you expect to pay for what you buy and work for what you earn.
When it comes to His undeserved love—His grace—you bring the same
thinking with you. God's grace, however, works differently. His grace is
yours, and it isn't possible to pay for it, earn it, or deserve it. God's grace
is yours, not because of you, but because of God.

....

....

....

....

....

....

....

....

....

....

....

ETERNAL APPRECIATION

Lord my God, I will praise you forever.
Psalm 30:12

Even in eternity, you will be thanking God. The appreciation of God's mercy by His people never stops. Without His grace, we would be forever separated from Him, lost in the cares of sin and a hellish existence. The bliss of a heavenly eternity could not be our inheritance. Could you thank Jesus too much now? Or could you ever find enough words to show Him your love? Maybe it's time to get started on your eternal appreciation of your Lord.

....

....

....

....

....

....

....

....

....

....

....

....

....

....

....

A LIFE OF JOY

You have greatly encouraged me
and made me happy despite all our troubles.
2 CORINTHIANS 7:4 NLT

Want to know the perfect recipe for happiness? Spend your days focused on making others happy. If you shift your focus from yourself to others, you accomplish two things: You put others first, and you're always looking for ways to make others smile. There's something about spreading joy that satisfies the soul.

SELF-CARE

Your kindness will reward you.
PROVERBS 11:17 NLT

What do you do when a friend shares her exhaustion or discouragement with you? Because you care, you probably listen, acknowledge her current reality, tell her how you appreciate her, remind her of recent accomplishments, or suggest she give herself a break. Today try sharing the same responses with yourself. Harsh words rarely motivate others—yourself included. When you're kind to yourself, you flourish inside and grow toward becoming the woman God designed you to be.

GODLY PATIENCE

Dear brothers and sisters, be patient as you wait for the Lord's return. Consider the farmers who patiently wait for the rains in the fall and in the spring. They eagerly look for the valuable harvest to ripen. You, too, must be patient. Take courage, for the coming of the Lord is near.

JAMES 5:7–8 NLT

I have to admit that one of the greatest challenges I face each day is the need for patience. I'm tested regularly on the subject, and too often I fail. Lord, I know I won't win this battle overnight, but with Your help, I'll daily work toward achieving godly patience.

....

....

....

....

....

....

....

....

....

....

....

....

A PERFECT FIT

*And you also are among those Gentiles
who are called to belong to Jesus Christ.*

ROMANS 1:6

Legos are fascinating toys. They come in various sizes and shapes. Some Legos fit anywhere. Others have specific functions and only fit in certain areas. Try to put them in the wrong place, and you wind up with either an awkward structure or one that tumbles. Lord, I want to be like that Lego that knows where it belongs. If I stumble down the wrong road, let me feel awkward so that I turn around before I fall.

EXPRESS YOUR HEART

I will praise You, O LORD, with my whole heart. . . .
I will sing praise to Your name, O Most High.
PSALM 9:1–2 NKJV

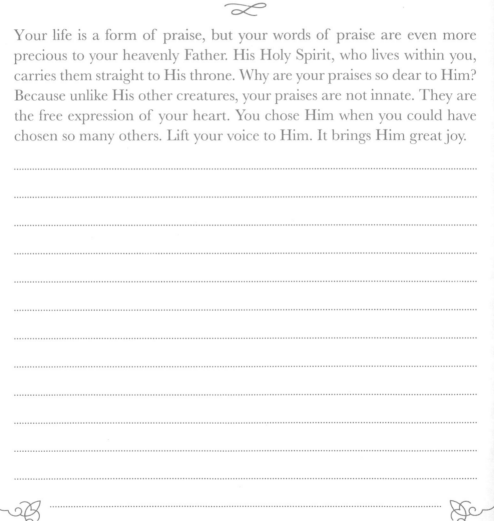

Your life is a form of praise, but your words of praise are even more precious to your heavenly Father. His Holy Spirit, who lives within you, carries them straight to His throne. Why are your praises so dear to Him? Because unlike His other creatures, your praises are not innate. They are the free expression of your heart. You chose Him when you could have chosen so many others. Lift your voice to Him. It brings Him great joy.

GIRLFRIENDS

*And our hope for you is firm, because we know that just as you share
in our sufferings, so also you share in our comfort.*

2 CORINTHIANS 1:7

Anne of Green Gables was right: Bosom friends are important. Girls—little
girls and grown-up girls alike—need girlfriends. God wired us to need each
other, to yearn for the heart bonding that results from sharing sufferings,
comfort, hugs, and giggles. Nothing's wrong with men of course, but they
don't make the same bosom friends as girls. Have you thanked the Lord
lately for your soul sisters?

....

....

....

....

....

....

....

....

....

....

....

....

....

EXAMPLE OF CHRIST

"The greatest among you should be like the youngest,
and the one who rules like the one who serves."

Luke 22:26

No matter what your role in life, you're a leader. Either your words and actions lead people toward goodness and virtue, or your conduct turns people away. God gives this advice: "Lead by being as happy to walk with the weakest as with the strongest. Lead by being as happy to serve others in an unnoticed, unsung capacity as to take center stage." Follow the example of Christ, who comforted even His enemies.

....

....

....

....

....

....

....

....

....

....

....

....

....

....

....

....

....

Day 167

SPIRITUAL TRAINING

All Scripture. . .is useful for. . .training in righteousness, so that the servant of God may be thoroughly equipped for every good work.
2 TIMOTHY 3:16–17

Did you realize that God prepares you to do good works every day of your life? Because you believe in Him, He will lead you to do good, following His plan for your life. How do you start? By reading the scriptures, His guidebook. There you will learn what to believe, how to act, and how to speak with love. Soon you'll be ready to put into action all you've learned.

JOYOUS PETITIONS

Take delight in the LORD, and he will
give you the desires of your heart.
PSALM 37:4

What are the deepest desires of your heart? Ponder that question for a moment. If you could really do—or have—what you longed for, what would that be? The key to receiving from the Lord is delighting in Him. Draw near. Spend time with your head against His shoulder, feeling His heartbeat. Ask that your requests come into alignment with His will. Then, with utmost joy, make your petitions known.

....

....

....

....

....

....

....

....

....

....

....

....

....

....

....

TEACHABILITY

Whoever heeds instruction is on the path to life.
PROVERBS 10:17 NRSV

Sometimes it's hard to take the time to heed instruction, although it would help you manage your current season more effectively. At your job, there's necessary training about new tech equipment. There's advice about health issues and information about how to better interact with friends and family. It's tempting to pretend you already know it all. Yet as a teachable woman of God, you can admit your need, accept sensible advice, and learn practical tools that will enhance your life today.

....

....

....

....

....

....

....

....

....

....

....

....

CHRIST'S LONELINESS

For He Himself has said,
"I will never leave you nor forsake you."
HEBREWS 13:5 NKJV

Lord, how alone You must have been in the garden when the disciples fell asleep. And when Your Father was forced to turn His back as You hung on the cross—was there anything to compare to what You felt? Yet You did it willingly. You understand when I'm lonely, and I thank You for being there during those times.

YOU'VE GOT A FRIEND

Whoever obeys his command will come to no harm,
and the wise heart will know the proper time and procedure.
ECCLESIASTES 8:5

I'm meeting a friend for lunch today. She's been a part of my life for two decades. Yet it's been almost a year since I've seen her last. How sad that life gets so busy that friends are times and dates in my appointment book rather than people in my daily walk. Father, You are the Friend who is constant. It's not hard to make time for You. You are time.

PRIORITIES

Seek those things which are above, where Christ is, sitting at the right hand of God. Set your mind on things above, not on things on the earth.

COLOSSIANS 3:1–2 NKJV

Human beings can be hopelessly shortsighted. But the person who sees past today and plans for eternity has both the present and the future in mind. When you accepted Christ's sacrifice for you on the cross and asked God to forgive your sins, your future in heaven was sealed. But the Bible also talks about laying up treasure in heaven. Place your priorities on those things that are eternal rather than on those things that are just for this world alone.

CAN YOU HEAR ME NOW?

But as for me, I watch in hope for the LORD,
I wait for God my Savior; my God will hear me.
MICAH 7:7

If there's anything more frustrating than waiting for someone who never shows, it's trying to talk to someone who isn't listening. It's as if she has plugged her ears and nothing penetrates. Mothers are well acquainted with this exercise in futility, as are wives, daughters, and sisters. But the Bible tells us that God hears us when we talk to Him. He shows up when we wait for Him. He will not disappoint us.

....

....

....

....

....

....

....

....

....

....

....

....

....

LIFTING LONELINESS

A father to the fatherless, a defender of widows,
is God in his holy dwelling. God sets the lonely in families.
PSALM 68:5–6

No one has come to take the place of the one no longer in your life, and you're not sure anyone really could. You ache with loneliness. These days are tough, and they're not days God wants to prolong. He sends people—relatives, friends, even strangers sometimes—to lift loneliness from you and bring you into the company and companionship of others. Ask Him to open your eyes and heart to those He sends to comfort you.

OVERCOMING THE SIN BARRIER

Godly sorrow brings repentance that leads
to salvation and leaves no regret.
2 CORINTHIANS 7:10

Godly sorrow comes when we feel the pain of our own sins. As we recognize our own wrongdoing and know that our actions have hurt us, others, and even the heart of God, we reach the place to do something about it. We repent, and God offers His salvation. Has sin come between you and your Savior? Turn at once in sorrow, and ask Him to make everything right in your heart and soul. You'll never be sorry you did.

....

....

....

....

....

....

....

....

....

....

....

....

A ROYAL VISION

Yes, joyful are those who live like this!
Joyful indeed are those whose God is the LORD.
PSALM 144:15 NLT

How wonderful to realize that you're God's child. He loves you and wants nothing but good for you. Doesn't knowing you're His daughter send waves of joy through your soul? How happy we are when we recognize that we are princesses—children of the most high God! Listen closely as He whispers royal secrets in your ear. Your heavenly Father offers you keys to the kingdom—and vision for the road ahead.

PUT ON TRUTH

Don't ever forget kindness and truth.
Wear them like a necklace.
PROVERBS 3:3 NCV

Perhaps like many other women, you enjoy receiving and wearing gifts of jewelry. That special gold necklace instantly transforms the simple black dress you've had for years. Living and speaking the truth with kindness and love is a little like wearing the perfect necklace. It feels, looks, and *is* lovely. Yet the truth isn't merely a nice accessory. It is an essential part of your inner life's wardrobe. Put on truth today and reflect the loveliness of God.

....

....

....

....

....

....

....

....

....

....

....

....

....

Day 178

RETURNING TO YOU, LORD

The LORD also will be a refuge for the oppressed, a refuge in times of trouble. And those who know Your name will put their trust in You; for You, LORD, have not forsaken those who seek You.
PSALM 9:9–10 NKJV

God, I am so weary of the bickering in our nation. It disturbs me to see people attempting to remove You from schools, courtrooms, and anywhere else they think You don't belong. They distort history and deny that this nation was founded with You as its leader. Heal us, Lord. Help us return to You!

NATURE'S WAY

*If any of you lacks wisdom, you should ask God, who gives generously
to all without finding fault, and it will be given to you.*
JAMES 1:5

As I sit at the picnic table and type, the hum of hundreds of bees attracts my attention. After a moment, the humming stops as the last bee enters the opening in the tree. That's when I really notice the storm clouds and distant thundering. The bees knew the skies were about to open up and unleash God-given rain. I pack up my laptop and head inside. The same God who gave wisdom to the bees also gave wisdom to me. Thank You, Lord.

RENEWAL

Create in me a pure heart, O God,
and renew a steadfast spirit within me.

PSALM 51:10

No two snowflakes are alike. No two sunsets are ever exactly the same. Your Creator delivers a masterpiece with every stroke of artistry He inspires. You are no different. With each touch of His hand, with every letter you read in His Word, He changes your heart from old to new—forming you in His image. You become more like Him each moment you spend with Him. Your Creator makes all things new—and He's continually shaping the perfect you!

....

....

....

....

....

....

....

....

....

....

....

....

....

CLOSE TO YOU

I stay close to you, and your
powerful arm supports me.
PSALM 63:8 CEV

There's an old saying, "I used to be close to God, but someone moved."
If God is the same yesterday, today, and tomorrow, He's not the one going
anywhere. So how do we stay close to God? So close that His powerful
arm supports, protects, and lifts us up when we're down? The answer is
prayer—as a lifestyle, as much a part of ourselves as breathing. Prayer isn't
just spiritual punctuation; it's every word of our life story.

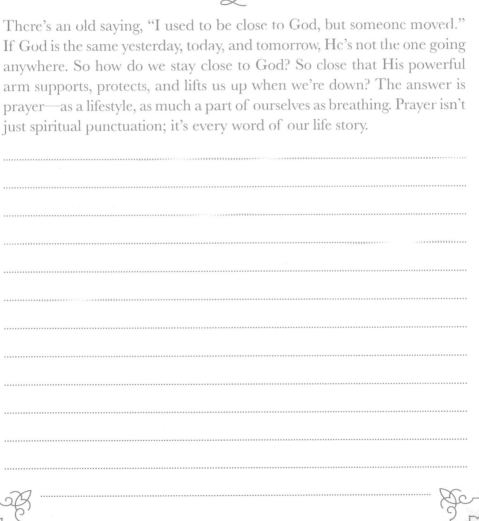

LOVE SHARER

He has made us competent as ministers of a new covenant—
not of the letter but of the Spirit; for the letter kills, but the Spirit gives life.
2 Corinthians 3:6

Caring for and comforting others is a profound privilege. With God's Spirit at work in you, let your everyday words and actions comfort and bless others just as God has comforted and blessed you. Your ministry makes you a love sharer rather than a lawgiver. Maybe you feel you have nothing to share with others, but you do. God loves you, and knowing that enables you to love others.

....

....

....

....

....

....

....

....

....

....

....

....

OUR REFUGE

The LORD Almighty is the one you are to regard
as holy. . . . He will be a holy place.
ISAIAH 8:13–14

When you live in awe of God—when He alone is Lord of your life—you have nothing to fear. If fears or enemies assail you, a place of refuge is always nearby. God never throws His children to the wolves. Instead, He protects them in His holy place. With Jesus as your Savior, you always have a peaceful place to go to.

Day 184

THE WAYS OF LIFE

" 'You have made known to me the paths of life;
you will fill me with joy in your presence.' "
ACTS 2:28

God gives us everything we need to make it through life. He teaches us His ways. Fills us with His joy. Gives us the pleasure of meeting with Him for times of intimate worship. What an awesome Teacher and Friend. He takes us by the hand and gently leads us from experience to experience, joy to joy.

....

....

....

....

....

....

....

....

....

....

....

....

....

....

....

....

A VIRTUOUS WOMAN

*A person's insight gives [her] patience,
and [her] virtue is to overlook an offense.*
PROVERBS 19:11 HCSB

"She never lets me forget it." Perhaps you've heard a statement like this from someone who's tired of being reminded of a past blunder. The purpose of the frequent reminder might be to help the offender see her error and never do it again. But it doesn't work. Instead, it causes shame, creates distance, and stifles reconciliation. A virtuous woman understands that nobody is perfect here on this earth and allows God to take care of the rest. That's freedom.

REACHING OUT

Charity suffereth long, and is kind; charity envieth not; charity vaunteth not itself, is not puffed up, . . . Beareth all things, believeth all things, hopeth all things, endureth all things. Charity never faileth.
1 CORINTHIANS 13:4, 7–8 KJV

God, I was just noticing all the people around me who really could use a friend. For whatever reason, they're alone and hurting. I need to reach out to them. I ask You to give me opportunities and ideas to let them know I care. Let me make the world a little friendlier for them.

THE MAKER OF DAYS

" 'You have made known to me the paths of life;
you will fill me with joy in your presence.' "
ACTS 2:28

The morning calls me. I stand at the back door and see the vibrant green grass. I imagine the fresh air and how it will feel on my skin. I have a book to read, and the refrigerator is stocked with sodas. Yet there is laundry to do, dishes to load, and groceries to purchase. Today I choose the responsible path. Tomorrow I may not be so dedicated. Lord, You are with me whether I toil or whether I dally.

....

....

....

....

....

....

....

....

....

....

....

....

INVITE HIM IN

*You, L*ORD*, give true peace to those who*
depend on you, because they trust you.
ISAIAH 26:3 NCV

Peace is to the kingdom of God what oxygen is to the atmosphere. Considering this truth, you may be wondering why you so often feel agitated and anxious. Think of it this way. Though oxygen permeates the air around us, we must breathe it into our lungs for it to do us any good. You must choose to let God rule in your heart. You must invite Him in. As you open your heart to Him, peace will follow.

....

....

....

....

....

....

....

....

....

....

....

....

Day 189

ONE NATION UNDER GOD

The poor are filled with hope,
and injustice is silenced.

JOB 5:16 CEV

"Give me your tired, your poor, your huddled masses. . . ," beckons the Statue of Liberty, offering a home and freedom to hurting people. Many of our ancestors flocked to American shores that were offering freedom of worship and an end to the injustice of religious persecution. May we never forget the sacrifices they made to pursue the hope of providing their children—you and me—with a nation founded on Christian principles. Let's strive to preserve that hope for future generations.

ROOM FOR PARDON

Happy is the person whose sins are forgiven,
whose wrongs are pardoned.

PSALM 32:1 NCV

Admitting guilt isn't easy for anyone. It's uncomfortable and embarrassing. But when we take full responsibility for our sins, God can bring us comfort and confidence. You too have made mistakes; we all have. The good news is that we aren't doomed by the mistakes we've made—not at all. With God, there is room for pardon. Tell Him about your mistakes, and let Him help you find a new beginning.

....

....

....

....

....

....

....

....

....

....

....

....

....

Day 191

APPRECIATION FOR MERCY

The LORD your God is a merciful God;
he will not abandon or destroy you.
DEUTERONOMY 4:31

Even when we fail God, He does not fail us. He knows our frailty and has mercy when we come to Him seeking forgiveness and wanting to change our ways. Mercy never holds grudges or seeks revenge, but it wants the best for forgiven sinners. So our merciful Lord calls us to make changes that show we appreciate what He has done for us. Is some appreciation called for in your life?

MERCY MULTIPLIED

*Mercy unto you, and peace,
and love, be multiplied.*
JUDE 1:2 KJV

Have you ever done the math on God's mercy? If so, you've probably figured out that it just keeps multiplying itself out, over and over again. We mess up; He extends mercy. We mess up again; He pours out mercy once again. In the same way, peace, love, and joy are multiplied back to us. Praise the Lord! God's mathematics work in our favor.

GENUINE WISDOM

The LORD gives wisdom; from his mouth
come knowledge and understanding.
PROVERBS 2:6

"Grow up. Gather the facts. Make wise choices." No doubt you heard similar advice when you graduated from high school and entered young adulthood. Even now your inner voice repeats these messages. But how can you experience genuine wisdom? Although you gain education through training and some maturity through experience, God is your source for wise and meaningful living. Enjoying everyday wisdom intertwines with knowing God intimately. Make deepening your relationship with Him your life goal.

Day 194

A DAY OF REST

*Six days may work be done; but in the seventh is the sabbath of rest,
holy to the LORD: whosoever doeth any work in the
sabbath day, he shall surely be put to death.*
EXODUS 31:15 KJV

You established a day of rest following Your completion of creation, God.
Although You expect us to spend time with You daily, You knew how much
we would need a day to retreat from our normal activities, to fellowship
with other believers, and to focus primarily on You. Help me never to take
this day of rest for granted.

....

....

....

....

....

....

....

....

....

....

....

....

MIRROR IMAGE

It is a land the Lord your God cares for; the eyes of the Lord your God are continually on it from the beginning of the year to its end.
DEUTERONOMY 11:12

The child seat in my back seat used to face the rear. I couldn't see my son while driving, so I purchased a special mirror that enabled me to see his reflection—to make sure he was safe. Then he hit the age and weight requirement for a forward-facing child seat. I purchased a special mirror that fits under my rearview mirror. It is constantly trained on him. Lord, just as I keep watch on my son, You keep us in Your sight at all times—to make sure we are safe.

A NATURAL RESPONSE

A kindhearted woman gains honor.
PROVERBS 11:16

As you grow in God, you begin to demonstrate His character and nature in your thoughts, attitudes, and behavior. Through you, His goodness becomes evident to others, and their respect for you increases. This will happen not because you demand it, but because it is a natural response to God's glory. For the same reason, you must respect yourself—casting down thoughts of inferiority and unworthiness. Respect God's presence and work within you.

....

....

....

....

....

....

....

....

....

....

....

....

ONE GUTSY GAL

*"It could be that you were made
queen for a time like this!"*
ESTHER 4:14 CEV

Crowned queen after winning a beauty contest, Esther was only allowed audience with her king when summoned. A wave of his scepter would pardon her from execution, but he was a hard man—and unpredictable. When Esther learned of a plot to destroy her people, she faced a tough decision. She was the only one who could save them—at supreme risk. God had intentionally placed her in that position for that time. What's your divinely ordained position?

....

....

....

....

....

....

....

....

....

....

....

....

....

....

EMBRACE YOUR POTENTIAL

"I have filled [you] with the Spirit of God, with wisdom,
with understanding, with knowledge and with all kinds of skills."
EXODUS 31:3

Have you reached your full potential? If you're still breathing, you haven't!
God has blessed you with a wide range of talents to tap throughout your
life. Enrich every stage of your life by following your interests, broadening
your knowledge, and developing your abilities. You will be surprised at the
variety of God-given gifts you possess—and experience the sheer enjoyment
of embracing your potential.

....
....
....
....
....
....
....
....
....
....
....
....
....

GOD'S FAVOR

May the favor of the Lord our God rest on us;
establish the work of our hands for us.

PSALM 90:17

Want your work to be effective? Don't make sure the boss knows every good thing you do. Seek God's favor, and He will see to it that your work really gets the job done, whether you're caring for a child, arguing a legal case, or waiting on a customer. Our Lord makes His people productive for Him as they serve others in His name.

....
....
....
....
....
....
....
....
....
....
....
....

FRESH MERCY

The faithful love of the LORD never ends! His mercies never cease.
Great is his faithfulness; his mercies begin afresh each morning.
LAMENTATIONS 3:22–23 NLT

Don't you love the newness of morning? The dew on the grass? The awakening of the sun? The quiet stillness of the day when you can spend time alone with the Lord in solitude? Oh, what joy rises in our souls as we realize that God's love and mercy are new every morning! Each day is a fresh start, a new chance. Grace washes over us afresh, like the morning dew. Great is His faithfulness!

....

....

....

....

....

....

....

....

....

....

....

....

WELL-DONE WORK

Committed and persistent work pays off.
PROVERBS 28:20 MSG

Make beds, pack lunch boxes, drive to work, answer phones and emails, shuttle kids, fix dinner, review homework, and start all over tomorrow. Whether you—or others—consider your work mundane or glamorous, at times it can feel boring or even insignificant. Yet satisfaction seeps into your soul when you whisper encouraging words to yourself. Try this truth: *God works. Jesus worked. I work. Even creation works. Well-done work reaps God-given rewards. He values my everyday work, so I will too.*

THINK ON PURE THINGS

Finally, brethren, whatever is true, whatever is honorable, whatever is right, whatever is pure, whatever is lovely, whatever is of good repute, if there is any excellence and if anything worthy of praise, dwell on these things.
PHILIPPIANS 4:8 NASB

There's just not much in today's society that encourages purity, but Your Word certainly demonstrates the importance of focusing our attention on things that are pure. From experience I have learned that life is more satisfying when it's geared toward pleasing You rather than the flesh, and I thank You for these lessons.

TURN THE PAGES

Your promises have been thoroughly tested,
and your servant loves them.
PSALM 119:140

Promises are made with words. You, Lord, are the Word. When we study Your Word, we are comforted and rejoice. When I read the story of Jesus at the cross, I am at a loss to comprehend the pain He suffered. But I know He suffered for me, so that I, a Gentile, could look toward a heavenly home. Lord, thank You that Your words are lined with promises for me.

GOODNESS OF GOD

You know that the Lord will reward
each one for whatever good they do.

EPHESIANS 6:8

Have you ever received a reward for an act of kindness? Maybe you returned a wallet or found a lost pet. So often the goodness of God goes unnoticed. He gives with open hands, never expecting anything in return because His motivation is love. He loved you enough to give up everything. You can give something to God. Become the rewarder! Let Him know that His grace and mercy have not gone unnoticed. Reward Him with your praise and thanksgiving.

CHERISHED DESIRE

*God our Father loves us. He is kind and has given
us eternal comfort and a wonderful hope.*
2 Thessalonians 2:16 cev

Merriam-Webster's definition of *hope* is "to cherish a desire with anticipation"– in other words, to yearn for something wonderful you expect to occur. Our hope in Christ is not just yearning for something wonderful, as in "I hope for a sunny beach day." It's a deep trust with roots that extend from the beginning of time to the infinite future. Our hope is not just the anticipation of heaven, but the expectation of a fulfilling life walking beside our Creator and best Friend.

RESTORATION

*" 'I will restore you to health and heal
your wounds,' declares the LORD."*

JEREMIAH 30:17

Have you prayed many times for God's restoring hand in your life, and yet you can't seem to get over those memories and emotions that cause you so much pain? God's healing sometimes happens overnight, but most often it takes time. Take comfort in knowing that each day in some small way, He is bringing you through, giving you strength, creating for you a future based on His love.

....
....
....
....
....
....
....
....
....
....
....
....

KIND WORDS

Let your speech always be with grace, seasoned with salt,
that you may know how you ought to answer each one.
Colossians 4:6 nkjv

Your words are a vital part of your witness. Speak to an unbeliever ungraciously, and chances are good that she will never forget it. But study and grow in the Word, then speak wisely and generously to others, and God can use your words to win them to His kingdom. People respond well to kindness and flavorful speech. What are your words saying today?

Day 208

JOY ON THAT GLORIOUS DAY

Yea, all kings shall fall down before him:
all nations shall serve him.

PSALM 72:11 KJV

There's coming a day when every knee will bow and every tongue confess that Jesus Christ is Lord. Does it seem impossible right now in light of current world events? If only we could see things the way God does! He knows that the kings of the nations will one day fall down before Him. Oh, what a glorious and joyful day that will be!

....

....

....

....

....

....

....

....

....

....

....

....

A CHEERFUL WORD

Worry weighs us down;
a cheerful word picks us up.
PROVERBS 12:25 MSG

Have you ever lain in bed staring at the ceiling and recounting all that went wrong during your day? The kids acted up at church, you didn't finish your to-do list, you missed an opportunity to help a neighbor, you disagreed with your mother. . .it all feels heavy. Try a new tactic with yourself. Instead of asking, "What did I do wrong?" ask "What did I do right?" A cheerful word to yourself will lighten your load.

GOD'S IN CONTROL

*"I am leaving you with a gift—peace of mind and heart. And the peace
I give is a gift the world cannot give. So don't be troubled or afraid."*
JOHN 14:27 NLT

Thank You, Lord, that You have a perfect plan for my life. I know I don't always understand it, but You know what's best, and everything that happens is for a reason—that You might be glorified. I'm so glad that You are in control and that I need not worry.

GOD'S HELPING HANDS

"And now, LORD God, keep forever the promise you have made concerning your servant and his house. Do as you promised."

2 SAMUEL 7:25

Sometimes we forget to let God be the source of strength in our lives. We think we must do it all ourselves. Father, no matter how much and how often King David stumbled, he kept his eye on You. Lord, remind us to never doubt the salvation You promised us. We march toward a better place.

THE HIGH PRIZE

*My sacrifice, O God, is a broken spirit; a broken
and contrite heart you, God, will not despise.*
PSALM 51:17

No matter where you've been, God loves you. He doesn't care about your past, but instead wants to give you an awesome future. You were worth the ultimate sacrifice. God gave all He had for you—at the highest cost. He cherishes you more than anything. You are the high prize that His Son, Jesus, was willing to fight and die for in order to restore you to your heavenly Father. Give Him your brokenness. It's a sacrifice you can afford to make.

....

....

....

....

....

....

....

....

....

....

....

....

Day 213

A LITTLE GOES A LONG WAY

*"The LORD our God has allowed
a few of us to survive as a remnant."*
EZRA 9:8 NLT

Remnants are useless by most standards, but God is in the business of using tiny slivers of what's left to do mighty things. Nehemiah rebuilt the fallen walls of Jerusalem with a remnant of Israel; Noah's three sons repopulated the earth after the Flood; four slave boys—Daniel, Shadrach, Meshach, and Abednego—kept faith alive for an entire nation. When it feels as if bits and pieces are all that have survived of your hope, remember how much God can accomplish with remnants.

....

....

....

....

....

....

....

....

....

....

HIS STRENGTH

I can do everything through Christ,
who gives me strength.
PHILIPPIANS 4:13 NLT

Has a new opportunity opened for you? Maybe after thinking and praying about it, you feel drawn to take on the project, but a nagging doubt holds you back. Are you strong enough? If you keep looking at your own strength, you will pass on the opportunity. If instead you look to God and realize that it's His strength He's offering, you can take on the challenge with confidence. In Him you have great strength!

WISDOM IN GOD

*Wisdom is the principal thing; therefore get wisdom:
and with all thy getting get understanding.*
PROVERBS 4:7 KJV

Have you ever thought of yourself as wise? The Bible says you can be.
You don't need a lot of education or a certain IQ. Real wisdom is found
in God. Simply obey your Lord's commandments and make knowing Him
well your first priority. Seek after wisdom, and you will find it in Him. As
you daily search for truth in the Word, your understanding will grow.

....

....

....

....

....

....

....

....

....

....

....

....

....

OUT OF THE PIT

I waited patiently for the LORD. He turned to me and heard my cry.
He lifted me out of the pit of destruction, out of the sticky
mud. He stood me on a rock and made my feet steady.
PSALM 40:1–2 NCV

When you've been living in the pit, you can hardly imagine being lifted out of it. The joy of knowing God can bring us out of even the deepest, darkest pit and place our feet on solid ground. Nothing is impossible with our Lord! If you're in a dark place today, call out to Him—and watch as He delivers you. He will establish your steps. Praise Him!

....

....

....

....

....

....

....

....

....

....

....

....

....

HEART TRANSFORMATION

As a face is reflected in water,
so the heart reflects the real person.
PROVERBS 27:19 NLT

Imagine sitting by a clear, cool stream and peering at your reflection in the water. You frown and the woman frowns back at you. You smile and the woman smiles. You chuckle and see the happy crinkle of your nose. Now take a moment to look inside your heart—at the evidence of God's love reflected there. Because you are a wisdom-seeking and God-revering woman, God is in the process of transforming your heart. Purpose today to reflect on this hope-filled reality.

SACRIFICE OF PRAISE

Give to the LORD the glory he deserves! Bring your offering and come into his presence. Worship the LORD in all his holy splendor.

1 CHRONICLES 16:29 NLT

Lord, may the life I live be a continual sacrifice of praise to You. You, who have done so much for me, ask only that I give my life wholly to You. How can I refuse? Let what others see in me be cause for them to glorify You too.

Day 219

FATHER KNOWS BEST

"God is not human, that he should lie, not a human being, that he should change his mind. Does he speak and then not act? Does he promise and not fulfill?"
NUMBERS 23:19

There's a country song that says "Sometimes I thank God for unanswered prayers." Its message is very powerful. It is saying that God knows what is best for us, and sometimes His answer to a prayer is no. Lord, thank You for having the wisdom to know when to tell me no.

....

....

....

....

....

....

....

....

....

....

....

....

....

SPEAK UP!

A person finds joy in giving an apt reply—
and how good is a timely word!
PROVERBS 15:23

Your life experiences speak of God's faithfulness and love, and He wants you to share what He has done for you with others. Someone out there may be struggling to take the next step toward God's love and plan for her life, and you can bring encouragement by sharing how God helped you through the tough times. In the process, your own faith will be strengthened. You have answers. Be bold and courageous. Speak up!

....

....

....

....

....

....

....

....

....

....

....

....

NAME ABOVE ALL NAMES

*O God, we give glory to you all day long
and constantly praise your name.*
PSALM 44:8 NLT

So what has God done that deserves our everlasting praise? His descriptive names tell the story: a friend that sticks closer than a brother (Proverbs 18:24), altogether lovely (Song of Solomon 5:16), the rock that is higher than I (Psalm 61:2), my strength and my defense (Isaiah 12:2), the lifter of my head (Psalm 3:3), shade from the heat (Isaiah 25:4). His very name fills us with hope!

SURRENDER YOURSELF

[Jesus said,] "If you try to hang on to your life, you will lose it. But if you give up your life for my sake and for the sake of the Good News, you will save it."
MARK 8:35 NLT

You may have thought about the concept of surrendering yourself to God, but you've hesitated because you want to be who you are—not a puppet of someone else. Don't worry! After all, God is the one who created you to be the unique woman you are. He has no intention of tampering with that. His goal is just to offer stability in your emotions and thought life and to enhance your talents and abilities. Surrendering to the hand of God means fulfillment of your deepest God-given desires.

LOOK AHEAD TO HEAVEN

*For our light and momentary troubles are achieving for us
an eternal glory that far outweighs them all.*

2 CORINTHIANS 4:17

What trouble could you face on earth that will not seem small in heaven?
No pain from this life will impede you there. Blessing for faithful service
to God will replace each heartache that discourages you today. When
trials and troubles beset you, look ahead to heaven. Jesus promises you an
eternal reward if you keep your eyes on Him.

....

....

....

....

....

....

....

....

....

....

....

....

....

....

JOY COMES IN THE MORNING

For his anger lasts only a moment, but his favor lasts a lifetime!
Weeping may last through the night, but joy comes with the morning.
PSALM 30:5 NLT

Can you picture a lifetime of blessing? Hard to imagine, isn't it? We think of "seasons" of blessing, but God continually pours out His favor upon His children. We have our ups and downs—our sorrows and our joys—but God remains consistent, never changing. We weep in the bad times and celebrate during the good. If only we could remember that on the tail end of every sorrow, there is a joyful tomorrow!

....

....

....

....

....

....

....

....

....

....

....

....

....

....

....

....

CAREFUL WORDS

*The good acquire a taste for helpful conversation; bullies push
and shove their way through life. Careful words make for
a careful life; careless talk may ruin everything.*
PROVERBS 13:2–3 MSG

What God created for pleasure and benefit can turn against you. God created food for your nourishment, yet too much or too little causes problems. Friendships add meaning to life, but unwise relationship choices bring unnecessary pain. God blesses you with work, yet job/mission obsession often causes burnouts. Similarly, words connect you with others, but reckless speech alienates. The good news: God doesn't leave you to wander carelessly through life. He gives you direction. Ask for what you need today.

....

....

....

....

....

....

....

....

....

....

....

....

EVENING RAINBOWS

Many, O LORD my God, are thy wonderful works which thou hast done, and thy thoughts which are to us-ward: they cannot be reckoned up in order unto thee: if I would declare and speak of them, they are more than can be numbered.
PSALM 40:5 KJV

When I first caught a glimpse of that rainbow, I was thrilled. When I really stopped to look at its brilliance, I was awed. Only You could have painted something so glorious across the expanse of the evening sky. Thank You for the beauty of Your promises.

....

....

....

....

....

....

....

....

....

....

....

....

PERSEVERANCE

You need to persevere so that when you have done the will of God,
you will receive what he has promised.

HEBREWS 10:36

Perseverance can be defined as "a quest to complete an idea, purpose, or task despite obstacles." Father, help us to run toward the fruit of the Spirit. The ideas, purposes, and tasks there seem so appealing, yet because we are human, we often get sidetracked by temptation. Help us to leave behind the ways of the sinful nature.

....

....

....

....

....

....

....

....

....

....

....

....

....

SPIRITUAL GROWTH

We all, who with unveiled faces contemplate the Lord's glory,
are being transformed into his image with ever-increasing
glory, which comes from the Lord, who is the Spirit.

2 CORINTHIANS 3:18

Each day, whether you know it or not, you are growing in the Lord, becoming more and more like Him. Simply because His Spirit dwells within you, you are being transformed from the inside out, reflecting the glory of God that burns from within. That's why you will often feel a nudge from deep down inside to deal with a certain issue or let go of a negative thought or behavior. You are literally growing up in God. How wonderful is that?

SOUL SISTER

"I always see the Lord near me, and I will not be afraid with him
at my right side. Because of this, my heart will be glad,
my words will be joyful, and I will live in hope."
ACTS 2:25–26 CEV

Laughter is the soul sister of joy; they often travel together. Humor is the primary catalyst for releasing joy into our souls and making our hearts glad. It's healthy for us too! Laughter is cleansing and healing, a powerful salve for the wounds of life—a natural medicine and tremendous stress reliever. Laughing is to joy what a 50 percent off sign is to shopping. It motivates us to seek more, more, more!

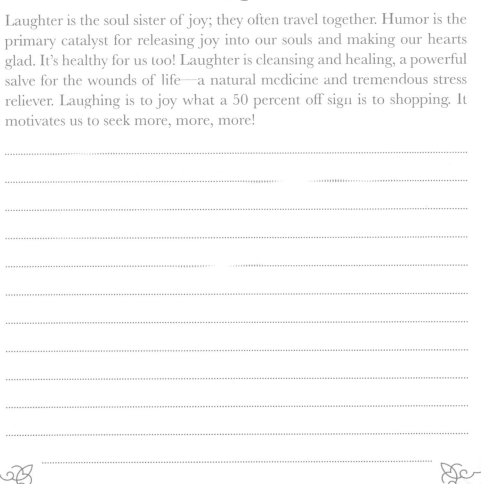

YOUR TIME

*There is a right time
and a right way for everything.*
ECCLESIASTES 8:6 NCV

Pure and simple, time is a gift. Each second, minute, hour, and day is yours to use as you please. *Not so fast,* you might be thinking. *All my time is filled with work and responsibilities and taking care of other people.* That's true—your time may be dictated by other choices you have made, but it is still yours. Ask God to help you squeeze in some time for yourself. He'll show you where to find it.

....

....

....

....

....

....

....

....

....

....

....

....

....

LOVE YOUR ENEMY

"But I tell you, love your enemies and pray
for those who persecute you."
MATTHEW 5:44

Without God's strength, could any of us follow this command of Jesus for more than a very brief time? Consistently loving an enemy is a real challenge. If you hurt from pain inflicted by another, you hardly want to pray for her. But loving actions and prayer can bring great peace between two people at odds with each other. For those who consistently follow this command, strife may not last forever.

LIMITLESS JOY

"I have told you this so that my joy may be
in you and that your joy may be complete."

JOHN 15:11

Did you realize that joy is limitless? It knows no boundaries. Jesus poured Himself out on the cross at Calvary—giving everything—so that you could experience fullness of joy. Even now God longs to make Himself known to you in such a new and unique way. May you burst at the seams with this limitless joy as you enter His presence today.

Day 233

SLEEP—ACCORDING TO GOD'S WORD

Hold on to wisdom and good sense. Don't let them out of your sight. . . .
When you lie down, you won't be afraid. . .you will sleep in peace.
PROVERBS 3:21, 24 NCV

Keep your room cool and dark. No caffeine before bedtime. Take a warm bath. Don't watch violent TV while trying to fall asleep. Listen to calming music. Contract and relax each muscle until your body feels less tense. These are a few of the instructions experts give to those who have trouble falling asleep at night. They often work too. Probably because they're based on good sense, research, and acquired knowledge. Just as God's Word advised many years ago!

AT PEACE WITH OTHERS

The fruit of righteousness is sown
in peace of them that make peace.
JAMES 3:18 KJV

There are a lot of people I must get along with. We come from a variety of backgrounds, and we don't always agree on everything. I've found, however, that peaceful disagreement makes for better relationships, so, Lord, help me to do my part to live peaceably with others.

THINK TWICE

Sin is not ended by multiplying words,
but the prudent hold their tongues.

PROVERBS 10:19

The weeping-willow branch used for switching retired to a corner well before the children of the household reached the no-longer-switchable age. Years later, one of the daughters finally asked why. The mother replied, "One day, while I was using it, it connected with my leg, and I realized how much it hurt." Lord, we often hurt others. And others hurt us. Only our weapon is words. Help us guard our tongues, because, Lord, when we use them to hurt others, we hurt ourselves even more.

REACH INSIDE

"The LORD is my strength and my defense; he has become my salvation.
He is my God, and I will praise him."

EXODUS 15:2

In the universe, there is really just one source of strength—God. Others may be strong for you on your behalf, but they cannot impart that strength to you. When you invite God to fill your heart and life, you are strengthened from within. His strength literally becomes your strength. You are empowered to do, to stand, to fight, to conquer. If Christ is there, you don't need to reach outside yourself for strength. Reach inside and find all you need.

AS THE TIDE TURNS

*"He will not falter or be discouraged till he establishes justice on earth.
In his teaching the islands will put their hope."*

Isaiah 42:4

Change. Besides our unalterable Lord, it's the only thing constant in this world. Yet the only person who likes change is a baby with a wet diaper. Isaiah prophesied that the Almighty will one day create positive change on earth. Like the tides that clean beach debris after a storm, positive change washes away the old and refreshes it with the new. In this we hope.

....

....

....

....

....

....

....

....

....

....

....

....

....

A SHINING LIGHT

*I consider that our present sufferings are not worth comparing
with the glory that will be revealed in us.*
ROMANS 8:18

When you suffer, it's hard to think of anything except your suffering, and that's why God provides something else to think about, something to balance the pain you are feeling now. Despite the circumstances of your suffering, open your spiritual eyes to how He is using the situation to reveal to you and others His presence and power. To break through the darkness of suffering, take your hope and comfort from the shining light of His unfailing love.

THE BEST ANSWER

Pray without ceasing.
1 THESSALONIANS 5:17 KJV

Haven't gotten an answer to your prayer? Don't give up. There's no time limit on speaking to God about your needs. It's just that we often work on a different time schedule from God. We want an answer yesterday, while He has something better in mind for tomorrow. So keep praying. God listens to His children and gives them the best answer, not the fastest one.

ANSWERED PRAYERS

But the angel said to him, "Do not be afraid, Zacharias, for your prayer is heard;
and your wife Elizabeth will bear you a son, and you shall call his name John."
LUKE 1:13 NKJV

Zacharias, though quite old, had been praying for a child for years. How funny that the angel prepared him by saying "Don't be afraid" before sharing the news! This answered prayer, though joyous, surely rocked Zacharias and Elizabeth's world! Have you ever consistently prayed for something without getting the answer you want? Ever felt like giving up? Don't! When you least expect it, your answer could come—and it just might rock your world!

....

....

....

....

....

....

....

....

....

....

....

FREE!

The fear of the LORD leads to life,
and [she] who has it will abide in satisfaction.
PROVERBS 19:23 NKJV

What ties you in knots, robbing your sense of well-being? Whatever it is that keeps you feeling trapped in a cramped little box and gasping for air isn't from God. Maybe you only feel like this occasionally. Perhaps you're accustomed to it. Either way, you don't have to stay in that box. God will open the lid and release you to freedom. Give Him your life, experience His power to free your soul, and enjoy the satisfaction He longs to give.

....

....

....

....

....

....

....

....

....

....

....

....

Day 242

ON BEHALF OF OUR SOLDIERS

When thou passest through the waters, I will be with thee; and through the
rivers, they shall not overflow thee: when thou walkest through the fire,
thou shalt not be burned; neither shall the flame kindle upon thee.

ISAIAH 43:2 KJV

There is a very special group of Americans whom I'd like to bring before
You, Father. They are our servicemen and women. So many of them are
in harm's way, Lord. They need Your protection in a way I cannot even
comprehend. Please put a hedge around them. Bring them safely home.

....

....

....

....

....

....

....

....

....

....

....

....

....

....

....

WASH ON MONDAY

May the God of hope fill you with all joy and peace as you trust in him,
so that you may overflow with hope by the power of the Holy Spirit.
ROMANS 15:13

I turn on the dryer, convinced that the clothes need yet another cycle. Fifty minutes later the timer sounds, and I open the door. I'd spent fifty minutes waiting in vain—nothing was inside the dryer. The clothes are still in the washer. Some people spin like that empty dryer. Time passes and they move, but nothing is really getting done. They are spinning in vain. Lord, we don't want to be empty vessels. We want to be filled with the goodness of Your ways.

SUCCESS STORY

Wisdom brings success.
ECCLESIASTES 10:10 NKJV

God has great plans for you. Sometimes your own plans may sound more adventurous or even more profitable than what God has for you. But remember, He sees and knows all—the beginning from the end. He knows the best road to take to get you to your destiny. He sees the obstacles along the way. He sees the eternal as well as the physical. Embrace the future He has for you, and you'll be a true success story.

....

....

....

....

....

....

....

....

....

....

....

....

....

LIVE AND LEARN

Lead me by your truth and teach me, for you are the God who saves me. All day long I put my hope in you.
PSALM 25:5 NLT

Acquiring spiritual wisdom is a fluid process. Trickles pool into mighty reservoirs from which we draw hope. God is right beside us moment by moment, day by day, guiding us, teaching us, feeding our reservoirs. But if we freeze the Holy Spirit out of our lives by apathetic or indifferent attitudes, the trickle solidifies into ice, and the flow of wisdom is blocked. Keep your mind open to God's everyday lessons and just watch the river surge!

OFFENSES

"I have swept away your offenses
like a cloud, your sins like the morning mist."
Isaiah 44:22

If you have ever watched the morning sun burn away the fog, recall the image when you come before God in prayer. Any offense against God you have ever committed—either intentionally or unintentionally—has been burned away in the light of His forgiveness. Offenses no longer cover you, and guilt no longer shrouds your heart. God has done this for you because He loves you. Respond in joyous thanksgiving today!

....

....

....

....

....

....

....

....

....

....

....

....

LOVE AND OBEY

"Whoever has my commands
and keeps them is the one who loves me."

JOHN 14:21

Do you feel you love God with all your heart? Then show it by obeying Him. Jesus paved the path for you. Through His own sacrificial life, He showed you what it means to obey the Father. A Christian who lives for herself, rather than God, shows wavering commitment. One who loves God wholeheartedly walks in Jesus' way, obeying His commands in scripture. Love God? Then obey Him too.

....

....

....

....

....

....

....

....

....

....

....

....

Day 248

JOYOUS PROVISION

*And my God will meet all your needs according
to the riches of his glory in Christ Jesus.*
PHILIPPIANS 4:19

Sometimes God goes overboard when it's time to make provision. He blesses us above and beyond what we could ask or think. He not only meets our needs, but He throws in a bit of excess just to watch us smile. If you're in a season of abundant provision, remember to share the joy! Pass on a portion of what He has given you. And praise Him! What an awesome God we serve!

DISCOVER BALANCE

Do you like honey? Don't eat too much, or it will make you sick!
PROVERBS 25:16 NLT

"All work and no play makes Jack a dull boy." (By the way, all work and no play can make Jill a dull girl as well!) You've probably heard this age-old axiom countless times. Yet the opposite is also true. All play and no work makes Jack *and* Jill uninteresting, not to mention unproductive. Focusing on one area of life to the detriment of its counterpoint is not wise. You *can* discover balance and thrive.

RIGHTEOUSNESS EXALTETH A NATION

Righteousness exalteth a nation:
but sin is a reproach to any people.
PROVERBS 14:34 KJV

I love the Proverbs, Lord, and one of my favorites says, "Righteousness exalteth a nation" (Proverbs 14:34). For many years our country has been powerful among its peers, and it's because You have been part of the lives of the people. We've begun to abandon You though. Please forgive us and restore us to a right relationship with You.

THIS IS THE DAY

"Give us today our daily bread."

MATTHEW 6:11

Yesterday's done, tomorrow is but a hope, today is unfolding before us. Father, let us appreciate the opportunities that come our way every day— opportunities to appreciate life, family, and You. Today is my day.

....

....

....

....

....

....

....

....

....

....

....

....

....

....

EXPRESS YOUR THANKS

Give thanks to the Lord, for he is good;
his love endures forever.
1 Chronicles 16:34

Each of the four seasons—fall, winter, spring, and summer—demonstrates creation's thankfulness to God for a job well done. The trees bow before heaven as their leaves fall gracefully to the ground. The glistening snowfall speaks of God's majesty. Flowers of every kind bow low to the glory of God in spring, and summer warms to the glow of all the blessings God has to offer. What has God done for you? Take a moment and express your gratefulness to Him in your own way.

....

....

....

....

....

....

....

....

....

....

....

....

....

....

....

....

....

WALKIN' BOOTS

I heard about you from others;
now I have seen you with my own eyes.
JOB 42:5 CEV

As children we sang, "Jesus loves me, this I know, for the Bible tells me so," and we believed because, well, we were told to. But we reach a crossroads as adults: Either pull on the boots of faith and take ownership or simply polish them occasionally—maybe at Easter and Christmas—and allow them to sit neglected and dusty in the closet. Have you taken ownership of your faith? Go ahead, sister; those boots were made for walkin'!

PERSPECTIVE

"My thoughts are not your thoughts, neither are your ways my ways,"
declares the LORD. *"As the heavens are higher than the earth, so are*
my ways higher than your ways and my thoughts than your thoughts."
ISAIAH 55:8–9

"We plan, God laughs." While the saying gets a chuckle, we're usually not
chuckling when our plans go awry. But step back and look at the situation
from another perspective—God's perspective. He sees your future as clearly
as He sees your past and present, and He knows how to get you from here
to there. Ask the Holy Spirit to help you look from God's perspective—and
laugh with the joy of knowing you remain under His watchful care!

....
....
....
....
....
....
....
....
....
....
....

PRAYER—GIVE AND RECEIVE

Brothers and sisters, pray for us.
1 THESSALONIANS 5:25

Do you find it hard to ask others to pray for you? Don't be afraid to take that step into humility. Paul wasn't when he asked the Thessalonians to pray for his ministry. Being part of the church requires an interdependence of prayers given and received. As a congregation prays for one another, their spirits connect in a new, caring way. Choose carefully those with whom you share private concerns, but never fear to ask a mature Christian to pray for you.

Day 256

JOY IN HEAVEN

*"In the same way, there is more joy in heaven over one lost sinner
who repents and returns to God than over ninety-nine others
who are righteous and haven't strayed away!"*

LUKE 15:7 NLT

What a party heaven throws when one person comes to know the Lord!
Can't you see it now? The angels let out a shout! The trumpeters play
their victory chant. All of heaven reacts joyfully to the news. Oh, that we
would respond with such joy to the news of a lost soul turning to the Lord.
What a celebration!

A RICH LIFE

The blessing of the LORD makes one rich.
PROVERBS 10:22 NKJV

God blesses His children—no doubt about it. Just look around you. Your life is richer because of His protection, provision, presence, grace, and love. How can you respond to God's blessing? Gratefully accept Him and all that He gives you. And then bless Him back. Perhaps that seems like the ultimate audacity. The perfect Blesser receiving blessings from His own creation? Yet out of your rich inner resources of blessing you can honor, revere, and bless the Giver.

WHO IS MY NEIGHBOR?

And above all these things put on charity,
which is the bond of perfectness.
COLOSSIANS 3:14 KJV

One young man asked You who his neighbor was, and You told him the story of the good Samaritan. I've always admired the Samaritan, but I sometimes find I'm more like the priest or Levite, finding reasons not to help others. How this must hurt You! Cleanse me, Lord. Mold me into a good neighbor.

OPEN ARMS

*"For the Son of Man came to seek
and to save the lost."*
LUKE 19:10

A toddler gets ready to go down the waterslide at our local pool. A mother stands at the top to situate him. A father is at the bottom to catch the child. Still, there's a middle section neither of them can reach. Lord, so many people in the world are at the middle section of life. They've gotten off to a good start—raised in the church. With open arms, people are waiting for them to come back to the church. Yet they're at a place in life where it seems the Word, the prayers, can't reach them. Father, lead them safely home.

....

....

....

....

....

....

....

....

....

....

....

A JOB TO DO

The desires of the diligent are fully satisfied.
PROVERBS 13:4

❧

Regardless of whether your work is in an office or in your home or in your home office, each morning when you open your eyes, you have a job to do. God is pleased when you apply yourself diligently to the task He has given you. It may be pleasant work—it may not be. Whatever it is, see it as your gift to your heavenly Father for the day. Do it as if He is watching your every step—because He is.

....

....

....

....

....

....

....

....

....

....

....

....

....

....

....

....

....

....

....

DO A LITTLE DANCE

*Then Miriam. . .took a tambourine and led all the women
as they played their tambourines and danced.*
EXODUS 15:20 NLT

Can you imagine the enormous celebration that broke out among the children of Israel when God miraculously saved them from Pharaoh's army? Even dignified prophetess Miriam grabbed her tambourine and cut loose with her girlfriends. Despite adverse circumstances, she heard God's music and did His dance. Isn't that our goal today—to hear God's music above the world's cacophony and do His dance as we recognize everyday miracles in our lives?

CERTAINTY

My son, do not let wisdom and understanding out of your sight, preserve sound judgment and discretion; they will be life for you, an ornament to grace your neck.
PROVERBS 3:21–22

You don't want to make the wrong decision, so you weigh the pros and cons in your mind over and over, spending sleepless nights wondering what to do. Now would be a good time to stop tossing and turning and put the matter in God's hands. Only He knows the outcome of all possible scenarios. Study His Word on the topic, bring to Him your best thinking on the matter, and open yourself to the guidance of His Spirit. Then make your decision with certainty and confidence.

YOU ARE VALUABLE

Who can find a virtuous woman?
for her price is far above rubies.
PROVERBS 31:10 KJV

Are you a virtuous woman? If so, you are truly valuable, no matter how unbelievers criticize you. Proverbs 31 says you can have a profitable life with good relationships, a happy home life, and successful business ventures if you run your life according to God's principles. So don't worry about the opinions of others if they don't mesh with God's. Instead, obey Him and be a valuable jewel to your Lord.

RESTORED JOY

Restore unto me the joy of thy salvation;
and uphold me with thy free spirit.

PSALM 51:12 KJV

When you restore your home, you return it to its prior state—its best possible condition. But is it possible to restore joy? Can you really get it back once lost? Of course you can! Joy is a choice and can be restored with a single decision. Decide today. Make up your mind. Get ready for the renovation to take place as you ask the Lord to restore the joy of your salvation.

....

....

....

....

....

....

....

....

....

....

....

....

....

....

....

....

....

....

Day 265

CALMNESS

Foolish people lose their tempers,
but wise people control theirs.

PROVERBS 29:11 NCV

Feeling angry doesn't automatically mean you've sinned. Anger is a normal response to injustice and wrong. God becomes angry over the disobedience of the people He loves. Jesus responded angrily to the corrupt money changers in the temple, but He didn't sin. It's when anger is allowed to rage or fester as resentment that it wreaks havoc with your soul and relationships. You're wise when you face your anger responsibly, discover its roots, and partner with God to control it.

....

....

....

....

....

....

....

....

....

....

Day 266

THOSE LEFT BEHIND

Yea, though I walk through the valley of the shadow of death, I will fear no
evil: for thou art with me; thy rod and thy staff they comfort me.
PSALM 23:4 KJV

Father, I'd like to take just a moment to pray for the extended families of
missionaries. We often forget that as obedient servants take Your Gospel
abroad, their relatives are left behind. The separation can be difficult. Ease
the loneliness. Bless each family member in a special way.

FINE OLD ROBES

Let the wise listen and add to their learning, and let the discerning get guidance—
for understanding proverbs and parables, the sayings and riddles of the wise.

PROVERBS 1:5–6

The main street of town is closed off. Cars, long past their prime, line the road. My husband's eyes light up. A vintage car show! What better way to while away a Sunday afternoon than studying the make and model of old cars? My Bible is opened wide. The saints of yesteryear line the pages. My eyes light up. Bible stories! What better way to spend an afternoon than studying the lives of Your apostles.

WHOLENESS

The very God of peace sanctify you wholly; and I pray God your whole spirit and soul and body be preserved blameless unto the coming of our Lord Jesus Christ.

1 Thessalonians 5:23 kjv

Human beings—and especially women—are uniquely complex. Emotions of the soul play on attitudes of the mind and together impact the body, which responds with enough intensity to affect emotions and establish attitudes. That's why it's important to be wholly surrendered to God. You must nurture and nourish every aspect of who you are. Ask God to establish harmony in a life, mind, and soul conformed to God's ways and a body that reflects inner peace.

GETTING TO KNOW YOU

*For the law never made anything perfect. But now we have confidence
in a better hope, through which we draw near to God.*
HEBREWS 7:19 NLT

Following Old Testament law used to be considered the way to achieve
righteousness, but obeying rules just doesn't work for fallible humans. We
mess up. We fail miserably. So Jesus came and provided a better way to draw
us near to God. He bridged the gap by offering us a personal relationship
rather than rules. Together we laugh, cry, love, grieve, and rejoice. We
get to know our Papa God through our personal relationship with Him.

A MIXED BAG

This is what the LORD says. . .
"I will comfort you as a mother comforts her child."
ISAIAH 66:12–13 NCV

Raising children is the most difficult, rewarding, exhausting, beautiful, chaotic, amazing job a woman can have. It's a mixed bag of dynamic emotions, pure affections, and unwavering devotion. When her children need comfort, a good mother instinctively provides it. God is the same way with His children. When you are hurting, He is there without fail, reaching out to you.

CELEBRATE YOUR NEWNESS

If Christ is in you, the body is dead because of sin,
but the Spirit is life because of righteousness.
ROMANS 8:10 NKJV

Know Jesus? Then your body and your fleshly desires are less important than your spirit. Because Jesus lives in you, sin has no permanent claim on your life. Though it tempts you and you may give in for a time, it no longer has a firm grasp on all your days. You can turn aside from it and dwell in your Lord instead. Celebrate your newness in Jesus: live for Him today!

....

....

....

....

....

....

....

....

....

....

....

....

Day 272

A COMPASSIONATE HEART

Break forth into joy, sing together, you waste places of Jerusalem!
For the LORD has comforted His people, He has redeemed Jerusalem.
ISAIAH 52:9 NKJV

Have you ever knelt to comfort a child as the tears flowed down his or her little cheeks? If so, then you understand the heart of your Daddy God as He gently wipes away your tears during times of sorrow. He comforts as only a Father can, bringing hope where there is no hope and joy where there is no joy. What a compassionate God we serve!

Day 273

CHARITY

She opens her arms to the poor
and extends her hands to the needy.

PROVERBS 31:20

Family, home, job, church, friends, school, personal and spiritual development—these fill your days. No doubt, like many other women, you find it difficult to become involved in long-term charity projects. Although you long to help, you only have so much time, energy, and money to go around. You can't do everything, but you can do something. Ask God to help you establish how, where, and when you can reach out to the hurting people in your world.

GOOD RELATIONSHIPS

Rejoice in the Lord always:
and again I say, Rejoice.
PHILIPPIANS 4:4 KJV

Thank You, Lord, for giving me a good relationship with my loved ones and children. So many people struggle with unhappy homes, and it's only Your grace that protects me from that. I ask that You'd keep Your hand on our home and give others happy lives as well.

LOST AND FOUND

"The LORD will guide you always. . .and will strengthen your frame.
You will be. . .like a spring whose waters never fail."
ISAIAH 58:11

After glancing at the map for the fourth time, I take a chance and rely on my gut feeling and turn right. I'm in a part of town I didn't even know existed. Sometimes I feel the same way about my Bible. Thank You, Lord, for providing us a road map that will never grow old or dull, and that constantly gives us new areas to explore and learn.

....

....

....

....

....

....

....

....

....

....

....

....

....

GOD WAITS

Be strong, and let your heart take courage,
all you who wait for the LORD.

PSALM 31:24 NRSV

God waits for you. You are the precious fruit of the earth, and as a farmer waits for harvest, God is waiting for you. Imagine what it must be like for Him to wait for you to grow, building trust and confidence in Him. He offers you spiritual food and water, believing that you will take root and become strong and confident in His Word and in your relationship with Him. And to Him, you're well worth the wait.

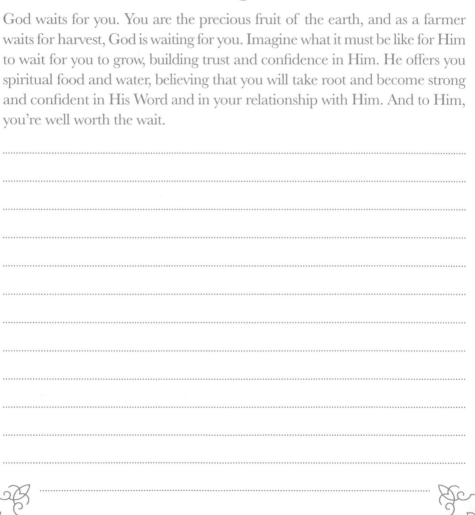

WORKING OUT

I will never give up hope or stop praising you.
PSALM 71:14 CEV

Praise is like a muscle; if we don't exercise it regularly, it becomes weak and atrophied. But if we flex and extend an attitude of gratitude daily, praise grows into a strong, dependable force that nurtures hope and carries us through the worst of circumstances. Like Helen Keller, who was blind and deaf, we'll praise our Creator: "I thank God for my handicaps, for through them, I have found myself, my work, and my God."

....

....

....

....

....

....

....

....

....

....

....

....

....

....

FOR YOUR ENJOYMENT

Give thanks to the L{ord},
for he is good; his love endures forever.
P{salm} 107:1

Do you regularly count God's blessings in nature—the beauty and variety of wildflowers, the immensity of the evening sky, the power of the ocean's waves, the majestic heights of a mountain? Even when you forget to say thank you, God surrounds you with these things every day. Name three things in creation you take pleasure in, and give thanks to God for each of them. Your God made them for you simply because He wanted you to enjoy them.

....

....

....

....

....

....

....

....

....

....

....

MERCY TRIUMPHS

Mercy triumphs over judgment.
JAMES 2:13

Not only is God merciful to us, but He expects us to pass that blessing on to others. Rather than becoming the rule enforcers in this world, He wants us to paint a picture of the tender love He has for fallen people and to call many other sinners into His love. When we criticize the world and do not show compassion, we lose the powerful witness we were meant to have. As you stand firm for Jesus, may mercy also triumph in your life.

....
....
....
....
....
....
....
....
....
....
....
....
....

THANKING HIM—PUBLICLY!

Give thanks unto the Lord, call upon his name,
make known his deeds among the people.
1 Chronicles 16:8 kjv

It's one thing to thank God in the privacy of your prayer closet; it's another to openly talk about the amazing things He has done in your life in front of a watching world. The words of your mouth, lifted up in joyful testimony, could have a powerful impact on those around you. So, go ahead—thank God publicly. Share the things He has done with people you come in contact with. Make His deeds known!

....

....

....

....

....

....

....

....

....

....

....

....

Day 281

DIRECTION

The human mind plans the way,
but the LORD directs the steps.
PROVERBS 16:9 NRSV

Your carefully thought-through plans may not play out as you envisioned they would. Life isn't predictable. Certainly it's not perfect. But one thing is sure. God knows the way through the good *and* disappointing times. He guides your steps, bringing opportunities across your path that will shape your character and help you become the wise woman you long to be. Let God direct you. He knows the way. He is the absolute best trail guide you could ever have.

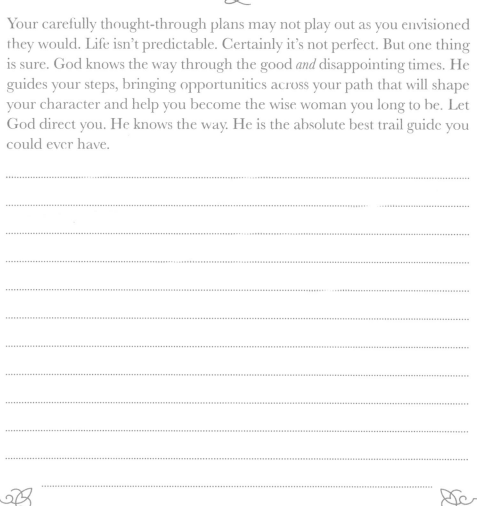

Day 282

FINDING TIME TO REST

It is vain for you to rise up early, to sit up late, to eat the bread of sorrows: for so he giveth his beloved sleep.
PSALM 127:2 KJV

I find it difficult to even sit down to a meal, Father. Resting seems like such a far-fetched notion. I know You want me to find time to rest and spend time with You, but I'm on the go constantly, and I still don't get everything done. Please help me, Lord, to make resting a priority.

Day 283

NO RSVP REQUIRED

Remember that at that time you were separate from Christ, excluded from citizenship in Israel and foreigners to the covenants of the promise, without hope and without God in the world.

Ephesians 2:12

At one time it was politically correct to use the term "melting pot" to denote the mixing of nationalities. Now we say "tossed salad." I'm not really sure what the difference is. I know only that at one time or another, we've all felt like outcasts. We've all looked through a window at a party we weren't invited to. We don't have to feel that way at all when it comes to God. We're all invited to the feast.

....

....

....

....

....

....

....

....

....

....

....

DIRECT YOUR THOUGHTS

When my anxious thoughts multiply within me,
Your consolations delight my soul.
PSALM 94:19 NASB

Your thoughts produce your attitudes and behaviors—your actions. They are, of all your physical assets, the most powerful. Your heavenly Father wants you to direct your thoughts toward life and blessing. The Bible says to think about those things that are pure, honest, true, virtuous, lovely, and of a good report. When you control your thoughts, they cannot be used by the enemy of your soul to harass you. Your thoughts will help you become free in every aspect of your life.

FOREVER JOY

We don't look at the troubles we can see now. . . . For the things we see now will soon be gone, but the things we cannot see will last forever.
2 Corinthians 4:18 nlt

A painter's first brushstrokes look like random blobs—no discernible shape, substance, or clue as to what the completed painting will be. But in time the skilled artist brings order to perceived chaos. Initial confusion is forgotten in joyful admiration of the finished masterpiece. We often can't see past the blobs of trouble on our life canvases. We must trust that the Artist has a masterpiece underway, and there will be great joy in its completion.

IN GOD'S EYES

Faith is the assurance of things hoped for.
HEBREWS 11:1 NASB

We human beings have plenty of insecurities, so you shouldn't be ashamed to admit you have a few. The good news is that you don't have to let them shape your life. When you place your faith in God, they will be replaced by the steadfast assurance that those things you hope for are yours through His love and grace. No more wondering if you're good enough or lovable enough or smart enough. In God's eyes you are perfect.

FLAWLESS WORDS

"Every word of God is flawless."
PROVERBS 30:5

Maybe you've had days when you've been tempted to doubt this verse. You wanted to go in one direction, and God's Word said to go in another. But if you were wise, you trusted in its truth instead of following your own way. After all, can you claim that your every word is error-free? No. How much better to follow in the perfect way of your Lord, who willingly shares His wisdom. To avoid many of the faults of this world, trust the flawless Word of God.

....

....

....

....

....

....

....

....

....

....

....

....

....

AN EAR TO HEAR

He that hath an ear, let him hear what
the Spirit saith unto the churches.

REVELATION 2:17 KJV

We need to "lean in" to the Lord on a daily basis. Listen to His still, small voice. Catch a glimpse of His vision for the church. Ride on the wind of the Spirit. Today, as you draw close to the Lord, listen closely. What is He speaking into your life? May your joy be full as you "tune in" to the voice of the Holy Spirit.

....

....

....

....

....

....

....

....

....

....

....

....

....

....

SAD OR HAPPY

*The person who shuns the bitter moments of
friends will be an outsider at their celebrations.*
PROVERBS 14:10 MSG

You can't predict what will happen next year or even one hour from now. Sometimes circumstances bring happy moments. Other times you get news that rocks your world. When you feel sad or mistreated, you'd rather someone empathize than discount your reality. If friends disregard your pain often enough, you'll probably hesitate to share much else with them, even your joy-filled times. God wants you and your friends to be compassionate with one another whether times are sad *or* happy.

GOD'S FAMILY

*Blessed be the Lord, who daily loadeth us
with benefits, even the God of our salvation.*
PSALM 68:19 KJV

As much as I love my family, I am infinitely more grateful to be part of Your family. To have other believers laugh and cry with me is a beautiful picture of Your love. To be able to pray with them, knowing You are in our midst, is great joy. Thank You for making me Your child.

....

....

....

....

....

....

....

....

....

....

....

....

....

KEEP THE INK FLOWING

For this is what the LORD says—he who created the heavens, he is God; he who fashioned and made the earth, he founded it; he did not create it to be empty, but formed it to be inhabited—he says: "I am the LORD, and there is no other."
ISAIAH 45:18

The drawer must have had a hundred pens in it! I decide it's time to do a thorough cleaning. I take out a clean piece of paper to test the pens on. Most pens no longer write. They look fine on the outside, but inside they're dry and useless. Lord, sometimes I meet groups of people who remind me of these pens. On the outside, they all look the same, but on the inside many are empty and only a few work. Please, Lord, never let my well run dry when it comes to serving You.

Day 292

A JOYOUS PRIVILEGE

Pray and ask God for everything you need,
always giving thanks.

PHILIPPIANS 4:6 NCV

Prayer is quite simply conversation with God. What a joyous privilege we have to be able to speak to the almighty God whenever we desire. How could you ever get enough of those times with Him? Meet with Him often to talk about your life. Tell Him your troubles, and leave your worries at His feet. Confess your sins to Him and receive His forgiveness. Tell Him how much you love Him and how grateful you are to be His daughter. He's always ready to listen.

....

....

....

....

....

....

....

....

....

....

....

....

....

....

....

DIVINE REFRESHMENT

"You were tired out by the length of your road, yet you did not say, 'It is hopeless.'
You found renewed strength, therefore you did not faint."
ISAIAH 57:10 NASB

By the end of each day, most women are ready to collapse. Tight schedules, relentless deadlines, and plaguing debts make our daily roads not just physically tiring but spiritually draining. How encouraging to know that renewed strength is available through the fountain that never runs dry. If we fill our buckets with living water—scripture, Christian music, inspirational books and DVDs—we will not faint but enjoy divine refreshment.

Day 294

WELL-BEING

The proof that we love God comes when we keep his commandments and they are not at all troublesome.

1 JOHN 5:3 MSG

If you have broken one of God's commandments and now see the reason for that commandment, you've learned an important lesson. Why repeat it? He has given you His commandments not to burden you with outdated rules and undue regulations, but for your physical, emotional, and spiritual well-being. Embrace all His commandments and obey them, and you will live in the full freedom He intends for you.

JOY WILL COME

*My lips will shout for joy when I sing praise
to you—I whom you have delivered.*
PSALM 71:23

Having trouble finding joy in your life today? Do what the psalmists often did, and remind yourself of what God has already done for you. How many ways has following Him blessed you? Begin by thanking Him for His saving grace, and joy will rise, no matter what you face today. Your lips will show the delight in your heart.

....

....

....

....

....

....

....

....

....

....

....

....

BLOOMING FOR ALL TO SEE

*Since God chose you to be the holy people he loves, you must clothe yourselves
with tenderhearted mercy, kindness, humility, gentleness, and patience.*
COLOSSIANS 3:12 NLT

Have you ever noticed that we're naturally drawn to people who are fun
to be around, people who radiate joy? They are like a garden of thornless
roses: they put off a beautiful aroma and draw people quite naturally. If
you want to win people to the Lord, woo them with your kindness. Exude
an inviting aroma. Win them with your love. Radiate true joy!

TOMORROW. . .

Always respect the LORD.
Then you will have hope for the future.
PROVERBS 23:17–18 NCV

Even for wise women of God, the future sometimes appears blurry. What do you do when circumstances change? When plans don't work out like you thought they would? When you lose something you cherish? There are no cookie-cutter answers. Yet as a woman with a heart for God, you can pause and remember when God has helped you in the past. You might even write these memories down. Now choose to let these previous times give you hope for what you'll face tomorrow.

NOW ENTERING THE MISSION FIELD

"You are the light of the world—like a city on a hilltop that cannot be hidden. No one lights a lamp and then puts it under a basket. Instead, a lamp is placed on a stand, where it gives light to everyone in the house. In the same way, let your good deeds shine out for all to see, so that everyone will praise your heavenly Father."
MATTHEW 5:14–16 NLT

There is a sign over the exit at our church that says, YOU ARE NOW ENTERING THE MISSION FIELD. You called it harvest, Lord, and You want me to do my part in gathering. Lead me to people who are prepared to hear and receive the Gospel. Let me be alert to opportunities to witness for You.

....

....

....

....

....

....

....

....

....

....

....

....

....

Day 299

EXTRA CLEAN INSIDE

"Sovereign LORD, you are God! Your covenant is trustworthy,
and you have promised these good things to your servant."

2 SAMUEL 7:28

The used-car lot near my home has vehicles lined up facing the street. Marketing slogans are painted on their windshields: LIKE NEW! FANTASTIC DEAL! My favorite description is EXTRA CLEAN INSIDE. I'd like to think that, as a Christian, I am extra clean inside, but I know the boast is false. Still, God, You bless me with the Holy Spirit and with the promise of good things.

FLOURISH!

The Lord sets prisoners free.
Psalm 146:7

Some women run from God, thinking He will ask them to surrender their freedom and lock them down to some religious regimen. In reality, just the opposite is true. Until we come to Christ for salvation, we are in bondage to our unwashed thoughts and sinful behaviors. Before we can flourish in God's kingdom, He has to remove our bonds. Fortunately, our heavenly Father is in the chain-breaking business. Ask Him to set you free.

....

....

....

....

....

....

....

....

....

....

....

....

....

....

....

....

TWO-STRANDED ROPE

The widow who is really in need and left all alone puts her hope in God and continues night and day to pray and to ask God for help.

1 TIMOTHY 5:5

Some women feel as though they are irreparably weakened when they are widowed. Where there once were three strands of a sturdy rope (his, hers, and God's), now there are two. But those who persevere through faith and true grit say the secret is to learn to rejoice in what is left instead of lamenting what has been lost. Look forward. Move forward. Keep that two-stranded rope strong, and never lose hope of a better tomorrow.

....
....
....
....
....
....
....
....
....
....
....
....
....
....

Day 302

PLEASING GOD

Our only goal is to please God.
2 Corinthians 5:9 ncv

When you have a specific goal in mind, you take every opportunity and use every resource available to you to reach your goal. The goal of living a God-pleasing life is no different. Look for opportunities in your day to do those things you know God wants you to do. Use the resources you have on hand right now to strengthen your faith, increase your understanding of His Word, and serve others with Christlike love in your heart.

SEEING GOD

No one has seen God at any time. If we love one another,
God abides in us, and His love has been perfected in us.
1 JOHN 4:12 NKJV

How do we see God? Often it's through other people. That's why it's important to have a compassionate Christian witness—people see you and think God is like you—if you claim His name. In that way, many people have gotten erroneous concepts about the Savior. But many more have come to love Him through faithful testimonies. Today you can love others and show them clearly what Jesus looks like.

Day 304

BEARING WITNESS

The life appeared; we have seen it and testify to it, and we proclaim to you the eternal life, which was with the Father and has appeared to us.

1 JOHN 1:2

We don't have to work hard at being good witnesses when we're walking in close relationship with the Lord. Our witness will flow quite naturally out of our relationship with God. In other words, we "are" witnesses simply by living the life He has called us to live. And by living the life, we point others toward eternal life. Now, that will cause joy to rise up in your soul!

....

....

....

....

....

....

....

....

....

....

....

....

....

....

QUIETLY GIVEN GIFTS

A quietly given gift soothes an irritable person;
a heartfelt present cools a hot temper.
PROVERBS 21:14 MSG

A knee-jerk reaction to an irritable clerk is to snap back. When a friend shoots an angry remark your direction, you may want to retaliate. However, when you offer the gift of a quiet response or understanding word, your generous act can diffuse the tension. Even a gift of time or money can make a positive difference. Offer homemade cookies or lunch out, or offer to take out the trash or help with a project. Your quietly given gift can cool a heated situation.

GENTLE PEACE

The LORD gives his people strength.
The LORD blesses them with peace.

PSALM 29:11 NLT

Thank You, Lord, for this opportunity to bask in the peace that You offer. As I sit here in the woods, listening to the creek gently bubbling over the stones, I am reminded of how Your presence in my life soothes even in the midst of chaos. I'm glad I have Your peace.

UGLY DUCKLINGS

"Why do you look at the speck of sawdust in your brother's eye and pay no attention to the plank in your own eye?"

LUKE 6:41

It is often easier to notice the flaws in others than to focus on their strengths. Why do we do this? Does it make us feel superior? Maybe it is because, like a red blob of paint ruining a fine portrait, flaws tend to stand out. They're easy to spot. Help us, Lord, to look past the stain and focus on the beauty—not only our own, but the beauty of others as well.

REAL FRIENDS

A friend loves at all times,
and a brother is born for a time of adversity.

PROVERBS 17:17

Tough times reveal real friends. One reason that is true is because real friends are the ones who stick around when things are troublesome and uncomfortable and not at all fun. But also it is true because when you are at your worst or weakest, you can only bear to be witnessed by real friends—those who already know you inside and out and accept you just the way you are. Ask God to give you that kind of friend.

GLIMMERING GOLD

*"So in everything, do to others what
you would have them do to you."*

MATTHEW 7:12

The Golden Rule. Most of us were raised with this basic guide to human relations, but sometimes the message gets turned around. Instead, we follow the Nedlog (*golden* backward) Rule: Don't do for others because they don't do for you. But Jesus didn't say to repay in kind; He said to pay forward. The actions of others are irrelevant. Regardless of what others do, we should treat them the way we'd like to be treated—with respect and consideration.

ULTIMATE SAFETY

*I've run to you for dear life. I'm hiding out
under your wings until the hurricane blows over.*

PSALM 57:1 MSG

When bad things happen, we tend to wonder, *Isn't God supposed to protect us from disaster?* Rest assured that your God knows and cares about what is taking place in your life, and His arms of comfort and consolation are there to enfold you in His love. All the while, His Holy Spirit is working in you to guard and keep your soul from anything that would threaten your eternal salvation. Hold firmly to God, and discover your immediate solace and your ultimate safety in Him.

LOOKS CAN BE DECEIVING

Therefore we do not lose heart. Though outwardly we are wasting away, yet inwardly we are being renewed day by day.
2 CORINTHIANS 4:16

On the outside, people see us getting older and frailer. But looks are deceiving. As Christians we constantly build our belief if we walk consistently with God. We're growing deeper in faith, being spiritually renewed every day. God's glory lies ahead of us, as on earth we learn to appreciate His love and compassion. Undaunted, we look ahead to eternity and a new body made perfect by our Savior.

A THANKFUL HEART

Let the peace of Christ rule in your hearts, since as members
of one body you were called to peace. And be thankful.
COLOSSIANS 3:15

Have you ever received really great news unexpectedly? Remember the inexplicable joy that rose up as you received it? You didn't conjure it up; the joy came quite naturally. Today the news is good! God loves you! He cares for your needs and surrounds you on every side. He is your defense. As you contemplate these things, watch out—joy is sure to fill your heart!

....

....

....

....

....

....

....

....

....

....

....

....

....

Day 313

ALWAYS THE SAME

GOD's blessing makes life rich;
nothing we do can improve on God.
PROVERBS 10:22 MSG

God is always the same yet never boring. He's continuously good, creative, kind, compassionate, and timely. He protects, loves, and guides you, your family, neighbors, pastor, and those missionary friends twelve flight-hours away. Every morning He's right beside you. He never walks out when you're talking to Him. Nothing you do can make God any better than He is. He rules the universe but knows what you're planning at 4:00 p.m. tomorrow. For exciting life adventures, partner with Him.

NO EXCUSES

Love your enemies, bless them that curse you, do good to them that hate you, and pray for them which despitefully use you, and persecute you; that ye may be the children of your Father which is in heaven: for he maketh his sun to rise on the evil and on the good, and sendeth rain on the just and on the unjust.
MATTHEW 5:44–45 KJV

I want to say, "You don't know what that person's like. He's impossible to love!" But You told me to love my enemies. You showed me how to do this by dying for me even when my life was loathsome from sin. I was hideous and unlovable, but You still cared. I have no excuse not to love my enemies.

WHEN IN DOUBT

He got up, rebuked the wind and said to the waves, "Quiet! Be still!"
Then the wind died down and it was completely calm.

MARK 4:39

Sometimes, Lord, I feel hopeless. I am so weak. I stumble. I cringe at the many sins I commit. Then, Lord, You remind me of Your disciples. Many were seasoned fishermen and, at sea, even they were afraid of storms. We are not worthy of Your grace, but our faith will lead us toward victory.

....
....
....
....
....
....
....
....
....
....
....
....
....

FRUITFULNESS

[Jesus said,] "Abide in me as I abide in you. Just as the branch cannot bear fruit by itself unless it abides in the vine, neither can you unless you abide in me."

<small>JOHN 15:4 NRSV</small>

You may think you aren't accomplishing anything in your life. Perhaps you work at a dead-end job or a disability has left you feeling useless and alone. No matter what your circumstances, God has a plan for you, and that plan is not out of reach. As long as you are looking to Him, your life will be fruitful and fulfilling. That's His will, His promise, and His plan.

....
....
....
....
....
....
....
....
....
....
....
....
....
....
....

WINGS

This means that anyone who belongs to Christ has become a new person.
The old life is gone; a new life has begun!

2 CORINTHIANS 5:17 NLT

Have you ever seen a butterfly crawling on its belly with caterpillars? Or trying desperately to hang on to its cocoon as it takes to the skies? Of course not—it spreads its wings and flies far away from its old life, discovering new and wonderful things it never knew existed. New life in Christ is full of discoveries and wonders, but you can't get there if you're still clutching the old life. It's time to let go, sister.

....

....

....

....

....

....

....

....

....

....

....

....

....

YOUR GREAT PURPOSE

We are God's handiwork, created in Christ Jesus to do good works,
which God prepared in advance for us to do.

EPHESIANS 2:10

Some people say life is merely a meaningless accident of nature. Perhaps the idea has entered your mind and thoughts too. If so, you understand why God in His Word declares repeatedly the value He places on human life. He created you out of His eternal love, and He has made you who you are and placed you where you are for His divine purpose. Open your heart and spirit to take hold of the great purpose God has for your life.

LIFE-ALTERING IMPACT

*We were therefore buried with him through baptism into death in order that,
just as Christ was raised from the dead through the glory
of the Father, we too may live a new life.*

ROMANS 6:4

Baptism is a picture of the old sinful nature's death and the new faith-life God gives those who trust in Him. Belief in Jesus has a life-altering impact. One moment a sinful person is dead, held in sin's grasp. The next she becomes an entirely new person, alive in her Savior. Only Jesus offers this glorious freedom. Has He given it to you?

A BIG SONG

Shout for joy to the LORD, all the earth,
burst into jubilant song with music.
PSALM 98:4

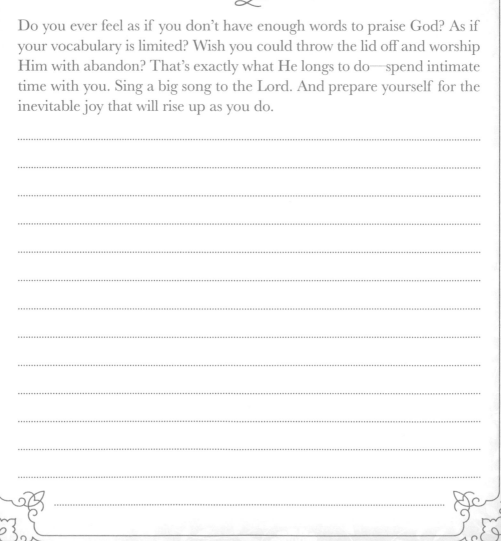

Do you ever feel as if you don't have enough words to praise God? As if your vocabulary is limited? Wish you could throw the lid off and worship Him with abandon? That's exactly what He longs to do—spend intimate time with you. Sing a big song to the Lord. And prepare yourself for the inevitable joy that will rise up as you do.

....

....

....

....

....

....

....

....

....

....

....

....

....

HEALTH

A cheerful look brings joy to the heart;
good news makes for good health.
PROVERBS 15:30 NLT

Medical experts indicate that it *does* matter whether you see the proverbial glass half-empty or half-full. Many believe that positive thinking leads to lower rates of depression, increased life span, and reduced risk of death from heart disease. Consequently, health professionals urge their patients to cultivate optimistic attitudes. Guess what? God recommends this also. Search for the good news in your life today. Make a list and display it where you'll see it often.

....

....

....

....

....

....

....

....

....

....

....

....

....

TRUE LOVE

For this is the message that ye heard from the beginning,
that we should love one another.

1 JOHN 3:11 KJV

Love—what a beautiful word! Yet many people are cynical about it, dear Jesus. I guess that's because there is so much artificial affection in this world. But I'd like for people to see true love—Your love—in my life. Please give me the ability to love as You do.

IN MY FATHER'S EYES

"For the eyes of the LORD range throughout the earth to strengthen those whose hearts are fully committed to him."

2 CHRONICLES 16:9

Recently, at a parenting class, I heard that if you really want your child to follow you, you should walk backward. So the next time we were at the park and my son wasn't inclined to follow me, I walked backward. Guess what? He didn't follow. He still went his merry way. Lord, I wonder how many times You walked backward, keeping me in sight and waiting for me to follow. Oh Lord, I am so thankful that You never give up on me and that I am always within the viewing range of my Father's eyes.

BEST DAYS

*I know the plans I have for you, says the LORD, plans for your welfare
and not for harm, to give you a future with hope.*
JEREMIAH 29:11 NRSV

Your age doesn't matter. Your looks don't matter. Your circumstances don't matter. For every individual, every life, God has a plan for the future. Even if you are reading this book from a hospital bed that you never expect to leave, God has given you a future. Don't drop out of life for any reason. With Him your best days are yet to come—better than you can think or imagine.

CHILL

I lie awake thinking of you, meditating on you through the night.
Because you are my helper, I sing for joy in the shadow of your wings.
PSALM 63:6–7 NLT

Are you a worrier? Do you frequently find yourself working up a sweat building molehills into mountains during the midnight hours? This passage suggests an alternative for that nasty and unproductive habit. Instead of worrying, try meditating on the loving-kindness of God. Like a distressed chick tucked safely beneath the snug wings of the mother hen, allow the joy of being loved and protected to relax your tense muscles and ease you into peaceful rest.

....

....

....

....

....

....

....

....

....

....

....

....

....

SPIRITUAL STRUGGLE

Put on the full armor of God, so that you can take your stand against the devil's schemes. For our struggle is not against flesh and blood, but against the rulers, against the authorities, against the powers of this dark world and against the spiritual forces of evil in the heavenly realms.

EPHESIANS 6:11–12

You cannot fight temptation on your own. Deadly spiritual forces work to pull you away from God and into the grip of sin, turmoil, and despair. Pray for a realistic awareness of the forces fighting against you, and let the Holy Spirit equip you for the struggle. Fill your mind and heart with His Word, dedicate yourself to listening only to the still, small voice of God inside you, and rely on His power and strength.

....

....

....

....

....

....

....

....

....

....

....

LOVE IS ACTION

Dear friends, let us love one another, for love comes from God.
Everyone who loves has been born of God and knows God.
1 JOHN 4:7

Want to see love? Look at God. Seeking love in this world is bound to be confusing. But in our Lord, we see the clean, clear lines of real love—love we can share with our families, friends, and fellow believers. Love for our enemies. Love for our Savior. Apart from God, we cannot truly and sacrificially love others. Love isn't just a feeling but the actions we take as we follow Him.

THE FRUIT OF THE SPIRIT

*But the fruit of the Spirit is love, joy, peace,
longsuffering, gentleness, goodness, faith.*
GALATIANS 5:22 KJV

Want to know how to have the ideal family environment? Want to see parents living in peace with the teens, and vice versa? To obtain a joyous family environment, you have to have a fruit-bowl mentality. Dealing with anger? Reach inside the bowl for peace. Struggling with impatience? Grab a slice of long-suffering. Having a problem with depression? Reach for joy. Keep that fruit bowl close by. It's going to come in handy!

Day 329

HEART

Tune your ears to wisdom, and concentrate on understanding.
Cry out for insight, and ask for understanding.
PROVERBS 2:2–3 NLT

Past generations seemed to emphasize the unemotional life approach. If you could see something with your physical eyes, prove it through scientific research, or touch it with your hands, it was considered valid. Recently there has been a shift to the "spiritual" side of human existence. But through it all, God hasn't changed. He has always cared about your heart *and* your intellect. Turn your thoughts and emotions over to God, asking Him for the understanding to make wise heartfelt decisions in your everyday circumstances.

LOVING GOD

*But the person who loves God is the
one whom God recognizes.*
1 CORINTHIANS 8:3 NLT

I say I love You, Father, although I'm not sure it goes as deep as it should. I want it to though. I want to be so in love with You that it shows in every aspect of my life. Help me to develop the intimacy with You that I should have.

....

....

....

....

....

....

....

....

....

....

....

....

....

VOLUME CONTROL

And because of his words
many more became believers.
JOHN 4:41

My husband likes the television volume set at forty-seven. I want it at seventeen. We settle on thirty-two, which means he can barely hear the words and I am covering my ears. Lord, it makes me think of the Sunday morning sermons. Sometimes the lesson is over, and I realize I barely heard a word. Other times the lesson is so powerful that, loud and clear, it seems to be directed right at me. Lord, we want to hear Your words. Keep us ever faithful. Never let us cover our ears.

....

....

....

....

....

....

....

....

....

....

UNMERITED FAVOR

By the grace of God I am what I am, and his grace to me was not without effect. No, I worked harder than all of them—yet not I, but the grace of God that was with me.

1 CORINTHIANS 15:10

Grace is often defined as God's unmerited favor. It means that His love for us, His care, and His concern are all free gifts—we haven't earned them. What a wonderful thing to be loved and accepted—just because! In God's eyes you are already pretty enough, smart enough, good enough to receive His best. He loves you for who you are. He wants you to become all you were created to be, but your relationship with Him doesn't hinge on it. What a wonderful word *grace* is!

EASY AS ABC

*God has done all this, so that we will look for him
and reach out and find him. He isn't far from any of us.*
ACTS 17:27 CEV

God is near. But we must reach out for Him. There's a line that we choose to cross, a specific action we take. We can't ooze into the kingdom of God; it's an intentional decision. It's simple, really—as simple as ABC. *A* is for admitting we're sinful and in need of a Savior. *B* is for believing that Jesus died for our sins and rose from the grave. *C* is for committing our lives to Him. Life everlasting is then ours.

....

....

....

....

....

....

....

....

....

....

....

....

....

QUESTIONS

On the day I called, You answered me;
You made me bold with strength in my soul.
PSALM 138:3 NASB

"What is this?" "Where are we now?" "How come this is this way?" One thing children know how to do is ask questions. Mothers know, however, that their children might not be ready or able to hear the answers to all their questions, so they answer the ones they can and tuck the others away. Your heavenly Father hears your questions—all of them. But He doesn't give you all the answers at once. Trust Him to know what you can handle. Ask in faith.

REAL SUCCESS

Save now, we beseech You, O Lord; send now prosperity,
O Lord, we beseech You, and give to us success!
PSALM 118:25 AMPC

Is it wrong to pray for success? No. But notice that the Bible connects success to God's salvation. Prosperity or any other achievement means little when it is separated from God's will and our obedience to Him. When you ask to attain something, do you also seek God's saving grace in that part of your life? If so, you'll have real success—spiritual and temporal blessings.

THE ROCK OF OUR SALVATION

*O come, let us sing unto the LORD: let us make
a joyful noise to the rock of our salvation.*
PSALM 95:1 KJV

God never changes. He's the same—yesterday, today, and forever. We go through a multitude of changes in our lives, but praise God, He's consistent. Doesn't that bring joy to your heart, to realize that the Creator of the universe is our rock? And don't you feel like celebrating when you realize that, no matter how much you mess up, His promise of salvation is true? Praise be to the Lord, our rock!

HELPING

Do not withhold good from those to whom it is due,
when it is in the power of your hand to do so.
PROVERBS 3:27 NKJV

The Bible provides a great basis for Sunday sermons about God and His plans. Yet it also includes nitty-gritty advice about acquiring people skills and cultivating a habit of bigheartedness. You can't assist everyone in this hurting world, but you can help in everyday ways: perhaps by carrying an elderly friend's heavy package, allowing a waiting driver into your lane, sharing pro bono business advice, or comforting a crying child. Helping is your personal privilege—and it's doable.

Day 338

GOD'S WILL FOR LOVED ONES

*For God is working in you, giving you the desire
and the power to do what pleases him.*
PHILIPPIANS 2:13 NLT

I've spent a lot of time praying about Your will in my life, Lord, but I have many loved ones who also need to know the work You have for them. Help them to be open to Your leading, and give me grace to accept what You call them to—even if it's not what I had in mind.

PAST, PRESENT, FUTURE

God sets the lonely in families.
PSALM 68:6

It's Friday and a holiday. I enter the hallway to my office, and silence greets me. Most of my peers have taken the day off. In the quiet, I find the time to do the little things I've been putting off. Yet without the banter of my coworkers, there's the constant feeling that something is missing. Lord, part of the joy of the Christian walk is the fellowship of brethren, the feeling that all is right. We thank You, Lord, for the friends who lead us, the friends who walk beside us, the friends who are yet to come.

SERVING

*[Jesus said,] "The greatest among you must become like the youngest,
and the leader like one who serves."*

LUKE 22:26 NRSV

Not everyone is called to be a leader, but if you feel God's call and sense
you have been given the attributes you need to lead others, you are right
to step out from the crowd and make it known. Just know that leadership
in God's kingdom is a position of service. As He did with Moses and King
David and Paul the apostle, God will humble you before He uses you. But
if you're willing and obedient, He may use you to change the world.

....

....

....

....

....

....

....

....

....

....

....

....

PRUNE JUICE, ANYONE?

Therefore, with minds that are alert and fully sober, set your hope on the grace
to be brought to you when Jesus Christ is revealed at his coming.
1 Peter 1:13

Diets are the devil. They exclude chocolate éclairs and hinge on effective use of that dreaded *S* word: self-control. In the fruit bowl of the Spirit, self-control is the prune. It's hard to swallow but nonetheless essential to our faith—especially where hope is concerned. If self-control isn't exercised, we can find our spirits soaring up and down faster than the numbers on our bathroom scales. Like eating prunes, daily use of self-control regulates us and prepares us for action.

CERTAINTY OF GOD'S LOVE

We who have fled to take hold of the hope set before us may be greatly encouraged.
We have this hope as an anchor for the soul, firm and secure.
HEBREWS 6:18–19

Without hope, you may feel as if you're being swept along by chaotic currents, unable to grasp anything solid. God wants you to know that He is about to reach you, lift you up, and set your feet on the firm ground of His Word and His promises. Though He might not reveal to you the reasons behind current circumstances, He invites you to place your hope in Him, holding firmly and securely to the certainty of His love and care for you.

GOD SAVES

I will give you thanks, for you answered me;
you have become my salvation.
PSALM 118:21

A new believer didn't write this verse. The psalmist thanks God not just for loving him enough to tear him from the claws of original sin; instead, this mature man of faith recognizes that God saves him every day, whenever he is in trouble. God does this in your life too. What salvation has He worked in your life recently? What thanks do you need to offer Him now?

....

....

....

....

....

....

....

....

....

....

....

....

....

REJOICING IN THE HARD TIMES

Yet I will rejoice in the LORD,
I will joy in the God of my salvation.
HABAKKUK 3:18 KJV

Perhaps you have been waiting on pins and needles for something to happen—a promised promotion, an amazing opportunity, something wonderful. Instead, you get bad news. Things aren't going to pan out the way you expected. What do you do now? Instead of giving in to disappointment, continue to rejoice in the Lord and watch the disappointment lift. He will replace your sorrows with great joy.

Day 345

INTEGRITY

GOD. . .relishes integrity.
PROVERBS 11:20 MSG

God cares about integrity. He wants you to be the same inside as you appear outside. Some may think this dilemma only shows up when someone pretends to love God but really doesn't. But there's a painful flip side that women encounter when they deeply desire God but live to please someone else instead. Fortunately, there's a cure. Courageously permit your heart to influence your actions, even when it's uncomfortable. God will help.

....

....

....

....

....

....

....

....

....

....

....

....

....

SPECIAL INSTRUCTIONS

*If ye keep my commandments, ye shall abide in my love; even as
I have kept my Father's commandments, and abide in his love.*
JOHN 15:10 KJV

Thank You for Your Word, Father. Without it I would be a helpless cause in regard to developing godly character. I'm so glad You preserved these special words that give me specific instruction on how to live. Help me to hide these scriptures in my heart so that I'm able to rely on them throughout my life.

....

....

....

....

....

....

....

....

....

....

....

....

....

SECURE THEIR HEARTS

*"All this I have told you so that
you will not fall away."*
JOHN 16:1

When they leave home, 75 percent of our young people will leave the church. I think back to my own youth group. It is as if a giant eraser had come down and rid the area of those who once were my buddies. So I guess that 75 percent is a realistic number. Lord, be with our youth; be with their parents; be with the church leaders. We pray that 100 percent of our youth will stay in the church. We pray for the future.

....

....

....

....

....

....

....

....

....

....

....

....

Day 348

ALL ALONG

*Your ears shall hear a word behind you, saying, "This is the way, walk in it,"
whenever you turn to the right hand or whenever you turn to the left.*

ISAIAH 30:21 NKJV

When we need answers, we often say that we are "seeking God." Yet because He is ever near, we need not seek Him. Nor do we need to seek answers from God, for He has already given us the answers we need. Instead, we need to seek to hear those answers, to tune out the busy thoughts and preconceived notions we carry with us. If you need answers, ask God to help you listen and discern, to open your ears to hear His voice that was there all along.

Day 349

TRUE COLORS

May integrity and honesty protect me,
for I put my hope in you.
PSALM 25:21 NLT

At first the raven appeared solid black, but when she perched in a shaft of sunlight, her feathers shimmered in iridescent emerald, turquoise, and teal: her true colors. We sometimes hide little acts of dishonesty—taking the bank's pen, pocketing that extra dollar from the clerk's mistake, fudging tax figures. But our integrity is on display at all times to the One who gave His life for us. When our true colors are exposed in the Sonlight, we want to shimmer too.

....

....

....

....

....

....

....

....

....

....

....

....

GO FORWARD

"You are a forgiving God, gracious and compassionate,
slow to anger and abounding in love."

NEHEMIAH 9:17

Perhaps the sin was huge and you're still suffering its consequences. Even though you feel deeply sorry for what you did and have apologized to those you hurt, guilt burdens your heart and weighs down your spirit. Do not let that sin continue on its damaging rampage through your soul. Instead, give your sorrow to the God who is bigger than any sin you could possibly commit. Be comforted by His promise of restoration and renewal, and go forward in forgiveness.

....

....

....

....

....

....

....

....

....

....

TURN FROM WRONG

There is therefore now no condemnation to those who are in Christ Jesus,
who do not walk according to the flesh, but according to the Spirit.

ROMANS 8:1 NKJV

No condemnation! What a wonderful thought for sinners! Forgiven, we know the comfort of having heaven as our ultimate destination. But have we also read the second part of the verse? This is no blanket agreement that okays sin. The joy of our freedom must lead us to turn from all wrong. Our Lord gives the strength to grow in Him.

JOYFUL IN LOVE

*Keep yourselves in the love of God, looking for the
mercy of our Lord Jesus Christ unto eternal life.*
JUDE 1:21 KJV

When you love the Lord and recognize His great love for you, it's easy to
be joyful! Think of His marvelous deeds. Revel in His overwhelming love
for His children. Recognize His daily blessings. May we never forget that
the Lord our God longs for us to see the depth of His love for us and to
love Him fully in return.

A LOST COMMODITY

What is desired. . .is kindness.
PROVERBS 19:22 NKJV

Have you noticed that kindness sometimes seems like a lost commodity? Everyone is in such a hurry. You hear recorded messages when you call for an important appointment. When you need help on the highway, it's often "tough luck." Then someone graces you with a spontaneous act of kindness, and your mood brightens. God knew that would happen. It's His plan. He treats you with loving-kindness so that you can share it with others.

CONSULTING CHRIST

"Now that you know these things,
God will bless you for doing them."
JOHN 13:17 NLT

Lord, often in my daily planning, I forget to consult You. Then I wonder why things don't work out the way I think they should. Forgive my arrogant attitude. I know that only as You guide me through the day will I find joy in accomplishments. Show me how to align my goals with Your will.

SNOW DAY

"Is this the one you say was born blind?
How is it that now he can see?"
JOHN 9:19

Snow fell. It coated the road and filled the terrain. Most drivers inched along at about twenty miles per hour. A few delusional drivers drove as if the roads were safe and visibility possible. Lord, how I talked to You during that drive when whiteness was the only color in my sight, when my hands were cemented to the steering wheel, and when fear gripped my heart. You were there.

Day 356

HOPE THRIVES

The LORD is good to those who hope in him,
to those who seek him.
LAMENTATIONS 3:25 NCV

Hope is amazing. It can grow and thrive even in the bleakest circumstances. A prisoner of war suffers brutal abuse at the hands of his captors, but they cannot break his spirit or rob him of the hope that one day he will be free again. It's hope that keeps us moving forward, always looking for a better day. Hope is God's gift. Thank Him for it by placing your hope in Him. He is profoundly faithful.

AIM HIGH

*My aim is to raise hopes by pointing
the way to life without end.*
TITUS 1:2 MSG

No woman is an island. We're more like peninsulas. Although we sometimes feel isolated, we're connected to one another by the roots of womanhood. We're all in this together, girls. As we look around, we can't help but see sisters who need a hand, a warm smile, a caring touch—and especially hope. People need hope, and if we know the Lord—the source of eternal hope—it's up to us to point the way through love.

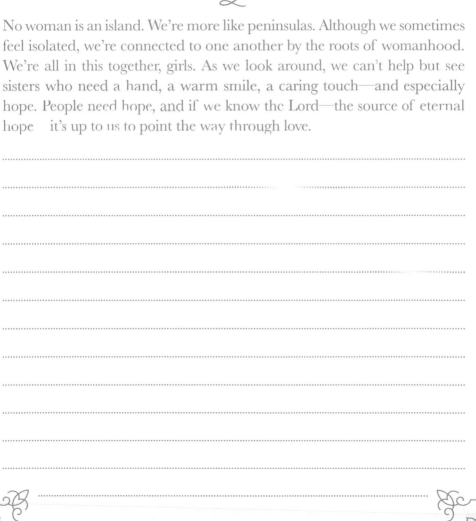

NOT THE END

Once made perfect, [Jesus] became the source
of eternal salvation for all who obey him.

HEBREWS 5:9

The older we are the more we understand the futility of this life. But there is great comfort in knowing that this life is not the end. Through His Son, Jesus Christ, God has provided a remedy for sin, with its constant menu of corruption and death. No longer are we headed only for the grave—but to the grave and beyond. This sacred belief is our blessed hope.

NOTHING IS IMPOSSIBLE

"For nothing will be impossible with God."
LUKE 1:37 NASB

The angel Gabriel spoke these words to Mary as he gave her the news that the aged Elizabeth would bear a child. God deals with the impossible in our lives too. We do not bear a Savior, but how has He helped us understand impossible relationships, juggle a hectic schedule, or help a hurting friend? God offers aid for whatever we face. Nothing is impossible for the One at work in our lives. What impossibilities can He deal with in your life? Have you trusted Him for help?

....

....

....

....

....

....

....

....

....

....

....

THE FORK IN THE ROAD

*What do people get for all the toil and anxious striving
with which they labor under the sun?*
ECCLESIASTES 2:22

Imagine you're approaching a fork in the road. You're unsure of which
way to turn. If you knew ahead of time that the road to the right would
be filled with joy and the road to the left would lead to sorrow, wouldn't it
make the decision easier? Today as you face multiple decisions, ask God
to lead you down the right road.

LAUGHTER

A cheerful heart is a good medicine.
PROVERBS 17:22 NRSV

The world is filled with trouble, stress, and responsibility. It can be pretty tough at times to keep your sense of humor and your positive perspective. Laughter breaks the tension and allows your body and soul to take a deep, healing breath. It lifts you up when everything around you is pulling you down. No matter what your circumstances, look for opportunities to laugh, and if you don't find any, create some of your own.

Day 362

GODLY EXAMPLES

So, my dear brothers and sisters, be strong and immovable.
Always work enthusiastically for the Lord, for you know
that nothing you do for the Lord is ever useless.
1 Corinthians 15:58 nlt

I've seen quite a few examples of godly people, and I'm thankful You've allowed them to cross my path, Father. It's a real encouragement to see other people who are becoming more and more like You. It helps me in my own quest for Christlikeness. Thank You for bringing these individuals into my life.

Day 363

AND FORGET

*The grace of our Lord was poured out on me abundantly,
along with the faith and love that are in Christ Jesus.*
1 TIMOTHY 1:14

I worry that if I'm not forgetting, I may not be forgiving. Can you have one without having the other? How many times can you profess forgiveness for an offense committed over and over? Oh Father, I am grateful I am not the judge—You are. I am grateful that You are the giver of grace—a grace I do not deserve but You give anyway.

Day 364

A PERMANENT CONDITION

A happy heart makes the face cheerful,
but heartache crushes the spirit.
PROVERBS 15:13

Happiness is elusive in this life. Because it's an emotion—like sadness and anger—it comes and goes with the circumstances. Joy is different. It's the permanent condition of the heart that is right with God. It isn't based on circumstances, but rather the known outcome—eternity with God. Forget about the pursuit of happiness and embrace joy. It will not fail you even in your darkest days and most trying hours. Rejoice!

....

....

....

....

....

....

....

....

....

....

....

....

SLATHERED IN SPF

You are my refuge and my shield;
I have put my hope in your word.
PSALM 119:114

These days the word *shield* evokes images of glistening sunbathers dotting beaches and carefree children slathered in sunscreen. Like the psalmist's metal shield, sunscreen deflects dangerous rays, preventing them from penetrating vulnerable skin—higher SPF for more protection. When we are immersed in God's Word, we erect a shield that deflects Satan's attempts to penetrate our weak flesh. Internalizing more of God's Word creates a higher SPF: Scripture Protection Factor. Are you well coated?

Scripture Index

MORE DAILY BIBLE INSPIRATION!

Everyday Bible Memory Devotional for Women

This fantastic daily devotional will encourage you to commit God's Word to heart, while devotional thoughts and prayers further reinforce the theme of the day's memory verse. *The Everyday Bible Memory Devotional for Women* is a great way to spend quality time in God's Word each day.

DiCarta / 978-1-68322-746-5 / $16.99

Everyday Bible Promises for Women

This book is full of scriptural encouragement, featuring Bible promises for every day of the year. Covering topics like Wisdom, Faith, Prayer, Encouragement, Love, Joy, and more—each scripture, devotional thought, and prayer speak directly to your heart, drawing you ever closer to your heavenly Father.

Paperback / 978-1-68322-685-7 / $7.99